HU

*Part One of
The Gabriels:
Election Year in the
Life of One Family*

Richard Nelson

BROADWAY PLAY PUBLISHING INC
224 E 62nd St, NY, NY 10065
www.broadwayplaypub.com
info@broadwayplaypub.com

HUNGRY

First printing: July 2016
I S B N: 978-0-88145-667-7

Book design: Marie Donovan
Word processing: Microsoft Word
Typographic controls: Xerox Ventura Publisher 2.0 P E
Typeface: Palatino
Printed and bound in the U S A

HUNGRY was first produced by The Public Theater (Oskar Eustis, Artistic Director; Patrick Willingham, Executive Director), opening on 4 March 2016. The cast and creative contributors were:

MARY GABRIEL	Maryann Plunkett
PATRICIA GABRIEL	Roberta Maxwell
GEORGE GABRIEL	Jay O Sanders
HANNAH GABRIEL	Lynn Hawley
JOYCE GABRIEL	Amy Warren
KARIN GABRIEL	Meg Gibson

Director	Richard Nelson
Scenic designers	Susan Hilferty & Jason Ardizzone-West
Costume designer	Susan Hilferty
Lighting designer	Jennifer Tipton
Sound designers	Scott Lehrer & Will Pickens
Production stage manager	Theresa Flanagan
Stage manager	Jared Oberholtzer
Assistant director	Sash Bischoff
Production assistant	Joseph Fernandez
Stage management intern	Kelsy Durkin

CHARACTERS & SETTTING

[Thomas Gabriel, a novelist and playwright, died four months ago, at the age of 64.]

MARY GABRIEL, 60, Thomas' third wife, and widow, a retired doctor.

PATRICIA GABRIEL, 81, Thomas' mother.

GEORGE GABRIEL, 61, Thomas' brother, a piano teacher and cabinetmaker.

HANNAH GABRIEL, 52, GEORGE's wife, and Thomas' sister-in-law, works for a caterer.

JOYCE GABRIEL, 53, Thomas' sister, an assistant costume designer, lives in Brooklyn.

KARIN GABRIEL, 54, Thomas' first wife, an actress and now teacher.

The kitchen of the Gabriel's house, South Street, Rhinebeck, NY.

Time: Friday, March 4th, 2016, 6 P M to approximately 8 P M.

"Like most other humans, I am hungry…"
M F K Fisher

for Bobbie & Cindy

(An empty room: the kitchen of the GABRIELS' *house. South Street, Rhinebeck, New York.)*

(Refrigerator, stove/oven [electric], sink; large wooden and rustic table used as a kitchen counter [with a drawer for silverware] is set beside another smaller table making an "L" shape; a bench with a back is to one side, facing the tables; a small desk; upstage a small cupboard. Chairs and a bench set upside down on the tables.)

(Exits: upstage to the unseen dining room; down left to the mudroom, back porch and back yard; down right leads to the rest of the house—living room [where there is a piano], the stairs to the bedrooms on the second floor, and to the front porch.)

(In the dark, Lucius' Wildewoman *plays through the main speakers.)*

*(*MARY, HANNAH, *and* JOYCE, KARIN *enter with trays full of kitchen objects. They will create the "life of the kitchen". They take the chairs and bench off the table and desk, and set them around the table and at the desk. They place a dish rack, dish towels, dirty dishes, glasses, napkins, bowls, a colander, pasta pots, etc. around and under the sink; notebooks, letters, catalogues, an I-pod dock, etc. on the desk;* MARY's *purse on the back of the desk chair; a timer, coffee pot, etc. on the top of the stove; a plastic trash can next to the sink; aprons on hooks on the refrigerator; oven mitts on hooks on the stove; fridge magnets on the refrigerator; salt and pepper, sugar bowl, cookbooks within bookends, a knife block, flour, sugar, a glass jar with reading glasses, a small tray of spices, a plate with the leftover crumbs from a sandwich, a mug for tea, etc.*

on the tables. GEORGE *too has entered, with a plastic box of old cookbooks; he sets some of the books on the bench and table, and the box on the floor by the bench.)*

(All but MARY *leave; the lights and music change:)*

1.
The Roosevelt Museum

*(Music [*Wildewoman*] now plays on the I-pod. The timer ticks on the stove.)*

*(*MARY *sits alone, having finished her late lunch, looking through an old cookbook. After a few moments, she takes her plate and mug to the sink, and washes them. She brings a cutting board from the dish rack and sets it on the table; turns off the music.)*

(The sound of the timer ticking is now heard louder.)

*(*MARY *goes to the refrigerator, takes out a towel-covered bowel, and brings it to the table. She takes off the towel; she flours the cutting board, and takes bread dough out of the bowl, puts it on the cutting board, and begins to knead the dough.)*

(After a moment, KARIN, *with a small paperback in hand, enters from the livingroom, startling* MARY:*)*

KARIN: They're back, Mary.

MARY: *(Startled)* What?! *(Seeing* KARIN*)* Sorry, I forgot you were here. What did you say?

KARIN: They just got back… You asked me to tell you.

MARY: Karin… Did you find something? What did you find?

*(*KARIN *hands* MARY *the book.)*

MARY: You found this. They just published this. Most are his old plays….

KARIN: I remember him writing one or two of those.

MARY: You do?

KARIN: In our apartment on Cranberry...

MARY: Karin, we've got a whole box of these. *(The book)* We don't even know what to do with them. Take it. *(Hands it to her)* If you want...Thomas would want you to have one. A memento.

(HANNAH entering with her coat on:)

HANNAH: You're still here, Karin. I thought you had to go.

KARIN: *(As she goes)* I do. I have to go soon. Thanks you, Mary. Thank you... *(She is gone.)*

MARY: You all were gone a long time. Take off your coat.

HANNAH: *(Explaining)* Now we're going to take a walk. Joyce "needs to get some air". She's had it with her Mom. You want to come? She wants us to sneak out the back...George is coming.

(MARY shakes her head.)

MARY: So how was the "all-new, remodeled" Roosevelt museum?

HANNAH: *(Shrugs)* It's what it now is...

MARY: What does that mean?

HANNAH: What has Karin been doing? I'm surprised she's still here.

MARY: Looking through the bookshelves. Whatever. She's been doing it for hours in the living room. *(Before* HANNAH *can say anything)* It's fine, Hannah.

HANNAH: You're baking bread.

MARY: I felt like making something.

JOYCE: *(Entering, having passed* KARIN*)* Karin's still here? *(She has her coat on too.)*

HANNAH: We were just talking about that.

JOYCE: *(Over this)* Is she staying for dinner?

HANNAH: *(To* MARY*)* She's not?

MARY: *(Over this)* No. She's not staying for dinner. I did not ask her to stay for dinner.

HANNAH: Good.

JOYCE: So you can say "no".

MARY: I know how to say "no", Joyce.

HANNAH: And I think you've done enough for Karin today. *(To* JOYCE*)* Karin just said she was about to go...

JOYCE: I've hardly said five words to her.

HANNAH: She didn't come to see you. Where's my husband?

JOYCE: He's coming. Getting Mom comfortable for her nap... He's prying himself loose. *(To* MARY*)* We're going for a walk—. Have you been out?

HANNAH: She doesn't want to go.

MARY: *(Over this)* The Stop 'n Shop... How was the Museum? I want to know.

HANNAH: I wasn't as bothered as Joyce and George—

JOYCE: It has really been fucked up, Mary.

HANNAH: *(To* MARY*)* She's slightly exaggerating.

JOYCE: Only slightly.

(The timer has gone off.)

JOYCE: I'm not even saying I was that *bothered*. Or even surprised. Why should we be surprised anymore? *(To* MARY*)* Your timer went off...

MARY: I know...

JOYCE: It's not what it *had been*. That's all I'm trying to say. It's very different. *(To* MARY*)* And— *(The second thing she wanted to say:)* Thomas would have really hated it. He loved the Roosevelt Museum. He loved the way it was. But this is the world we now live in.

MARY: I'm happy I didn't go then...I'd like to remember that museum the way *Thomas* liked it.

*(*MARY *washes the bowl in the sink.)*

HANNAH: You need any help?

*(*MARY *shakes her head and will go to the cupboard to get a bread pan.)*

MARY: What did they do to it?

JOYCE: The museum? Everything. You feel they are *pushing* things on you now. Like you can't think for yourself anymore. I'm sure it's what the Bush libraries are like. In *Texas*.

HANNAH: I'll bet you the Bush libraries are even worse, Joyce.

*(*MARY *will get butter out of the refrigerator, and will butter the bottom and sides of the pan as:)*

JOYCE: *(To* MARY*)* Mom seemed to enjoy herself though.

MARY: Good.

*(*GEORGE *enters from the living room still in his coat.)*

HANNAH: Here comes my husband...

JOYCE: Come on, let's go. Let's get some air.

GEORGE: Why is Karin still here?

HANNAH: *(Over the end of this)* She's not staying for dinner.

JOYCE: *(To* GEORGE*)* Let's go.

GEORGE: You go. I'm going to stay.

JOYCE: What? Why? *(Confused:)* Mom in bed? She taking her nap?

GEORGE: *(Hesitates, then)* Not yet...

JOYCE: What?? Are you kidding me, George?

GEORGE: *(Over this)* Joyce, she decided...

JOYCE: What?? What has Mom decided now? What the hell is she deciding now?

HANNAH: Joyce—

. GEORGE: She decided she doesn't need a nap.

JOYCE: *(It just comes out:)* No.

GEORGE: She says she wants to stay up.

JOYCE: No. Please god, no. I knew this would happen.

GEORGE: Joyce—

JOYCE: *(Defensive)* She's tired, that's all what I mean. I'm thinking of her...I am...

HANNAH: *(To GEORGE)* I'm sure she is.

JOYCE: *(To GEORGE)* She looks exhausted... She should be in bed. *(To the others)* Or am I wrong? Tell me I'm wrong. *(To MARY, defensive)* I had to help her up the porch steps.

HANNAH: I think she just lets us do that, Joyce.

MARY: She does "let" you do that... *(She shapes the bread dough into a loaf and puts it in the bread pan.)*

JOYCE: I don't think so.

GEORGE: *(To JOYCE)* You want to tell her to take a nap? Go ahead and tell her. *I* told her. [points] She's right in there, in her chair...

JOYCE: I guess then we're *not* taking a walk... *(She starts to take off her coat. To GEORGE)* If she doesn't take her nap now, she's going to...

(HANNAH *is taking off her coat.*)

GEORGE: She's going to what? She'll be fine.

(MARY *will take the cutting board, etc. to the sink and wash them.*)

HANNAH: *(With her coat, to* JOYCE*)* Give me your coat. I'll hang it up.

JOYCE: *(To* GEORGE*)* Mom looked absolutely exhausted. That's all I was saying.

MARY: I'm sure, today wore her out.

JOYCE: *(Over this)* She had to see everything. I mean every *thing*. She sat down on every goddamn bench. We must have been in there five hours...

MARY: She's old.

JOYCE: Thanks for that news.... *(Trying to explain)* I haven't been here like you, so...

HANNAH: I'm sure each time there's a bit of a— surprise...

GEORGE: You could have come for Christmas, Joyce.

MARY: *(To* GEORGE*)* She had just been here.

JOYCE: I had just been here.

(GEORGE *now tries to hand hannah his coat.*)

JOYCE: *(To* GEORGE, *incredulous)* Hang up your own coat. She's not your servant...

(GEORGE *starts to put his coat on a chair.*)

JOYCE: Don't leave it there. That's a chair.
There are *hooks*... The same hooks that have been out in that hallway forever.

GEORGE: I know where the hooks are.

HANNAH: Give me the coat. I'll hang it up.

JOYCE: Don't spoil him, Hannah. He's spoiled enough.

MARY: Joyce...

HANNAH: Joyce, the other night—

GEORGE: *(To* HANNAH*)* What??

HANNAH: *(Three coats in her arms)* The other night we're watching a film. Japanese.

GEORGE: I was joking, Hannah. Come on.

HANNAH: *(Over this)* And this guy comes home, in the film, and slips off his shoes; the wife hurries to get his robe, and as he takes off his jacket he just drops it on the floor. Just drops it.

GEORGE: I was teasing... She'll believe you.

HANNAH: The wife's standing right there. So she has to reach down and pick it up. George turns to me and says— "see".

JOYCE: *("Outraged")* Oh for Christ sake... That's embarrassing. She's your wife not your slave.

MARY: He was kidding...

HANNAH: *(To* GEORGE, *as she heads off)* I know you were joking...

GEORGE: Then why tell the story?

HANNAH: Because it's funny. *(She goes off with the coats.)*

*(*MARY *wipes the table.)*

MARY: *(To say something)* Did you have any lunch? I think there are still some cold cuts...

GEORGE: We ate at the EverReady. Even got a booth right away. *(Then)* My brother loved the Roosevelt Museum. Thomas did some research in that library, didn't he? Or am I wrong?

JOYCE: For his Roosevelt play?

GEORGE: The last thing you're faced with, just before you leave? There's a movie—with—guess whose voice on it, Mary? *Bill Clinton's.*

(HANNAH *enters having heard this:*)

HANNAH: You didn't let her guess.

MARY: That's not *F D R.*

GEORGE: *(Emphatic)* No.

HANNAH: *(Shrugs)* He was a president...

MARY: I was going to guess Hillary.

JOYCE: Not Trump?

GEORGE: *(Over this)* You used to be able to walk in there and you felt you were in the presence of *that man.*

HANNAH: *(To* MARY*)* You should go, see for yourself.

GEORGE: *(Continuing, over this)* It's about what *they* want you to believe. To think. They feel they need to tell you what to think. So that you'll vote for us *Democrats?* It's not history anymore, it's now just politics. What the hell happened to history?

JOYCE: *(To* GEORGE*)* So where did you leave Mom? If she didn't go upstairs to take a nap. You know—she's probably sick of us too.

MARY: I doubt if your mother—

JOYCE: *(Hearing herself)* I mean—

GEORGE: *(Be quiet:)* Joyce...

JOYCE: Mom can't hear. She can't hear if you're sitting right next to her...

GEORGE: *(Answering the question)* She was still in her chair, in the living room.

HANNAH: I peeked in. She's talking to Karin...

JOYCE: *At* Karin is more like it. So poor Karin got trapped...

HANNAH: It sounded like she was telling Karin about her voting for Roosevelt.

JOYCE: Is that even possible?

GEORGE: Who knows? Why Karin? *(Answers his own question)* Because she's polite and still listens… Should we go and rescue Karin?

JOYCE: *(To MARY)* Hannah told us at lunch, you don't remember actually inviting her…

MARY: I must have.

JOYCE: I don't think I've seen her in decades.

GEORGE: She was at Thomas' memorial in the city.

JOYCE: I wasn't looking for her then.

HANNAH: She visited in October. Thomas asked Mary to get in touch…

JOYCE: Did he? Maybe I knew that… Huh. *(To MARY)* You okay with that?

HANNAH: She seemed really "pleased" to be there. This morning… So—we all did a nice thing.

(No one knows what to do, where to go; they watch MARY work.)

MARY: I just felt like *making* something…

GEORGE: Makes sense.

HANNAH: *(Trying to make a joke)* I wake up like that sometimes too. Then I don't make anything. *(To GEORGE)* Do I?

GEORGE: Yes, you do…

(JOYCE is looking into the coffeepot on the stove.)

MARY: I should make a fresh pot, Joyce.

JOYCE: It's still—sort of warm. I'm going to buy this house a coffee maker. They cost like ten bucks. *(She will take a cup from the dishrack.)*

GEORGE: *(To* JOYCE*)* You going to stay tonight in my room? Your old room's full of crap—

MARY: I made up a bed in George and Thomas' old room…

JOYCE: I don't care where I sleep.

*(*KARIN *appears in the doorway from the living room:)*

JOYCE: Look, she's escaped. Good for you. Good for Karin.

KARIN: *(Over the end)* I wasn't escaping.

GEORGE: *(Over this)* My sister's always joking.

KARIN: *(To* MARY*)* Patricia wonders if she could get a cup of tea. I could do that. Just tell me where you keep the tea, Mary…

JOYCE: Karin—my mother means: go and get [George and herself] her "children", and make them come back in there. That's what she means—by "cup-of-tea". It's code. *(To* GEORGE*)* Isn't it?

GEORGE: That is what our mother means…

HANNAH: *(To* KARIN*)* Sit down. Join us…

JOYCE: *(A joke)* You're safe in here.

*(*KARIN *will sit at the table.)*

KARIN: *(Confused)* What do you mean?

HANNAH: *(To* KARIN*)* So their Mom voted for Roosevelt?

KARIN: At least five times she said.

(As JOYCE *pours her coffee:)*

MARY: I'm going to make a new pot… That's not even hot—

*(*MARY *will empty the pot in the sink; take out the grounds, wash the pot; get water from the sink, coffee from the freezer, and start to make coffee as…)*

GEORGE: (*To* HANNAH *to say something*) Mary was surprised we got a table right away at the EverReady.

HANNAH: Unlike last night.

JOYCE: What happened last—?

HANNAH: (*Over this*) We wanted to go out for dinner. And how rare is that?

KARIN: (*Standing there, interrupts*) I should probably be going soon...

MARY: Do you have to go already?

KARIN: I guess not. I'm not in the way?

MARY: No. Of course not. (*pointing to the bench*) Karin, all those books were Thomas' too. Research for something. I thought they belonged in here. You'll see why. Take a look.

(KARIN *will sit on the bench and look through the books.*)

HANNAH: (*Continues to* JOYCE) Every place in Rhinebeck village, packed to the gills. On a *Thursday* night. One place even laughed at me... "Oh we're usually booked out from Wednesday..."

JOYCE: In Rhinebeck?? When did that happen?

HANNAH: It happened. When? We don't know. We never go out...

GEORGE: Joyce...Mom's in there all by herself...

JOYCE: I'm almost done. (*She takes a sip of her coffee.*)

MARY: (*Ready to put in the scoops of coffee*) How much am I making? Who's going to want coffee? (*No one does*) Then what am I making it for?

HANNAH: (*To* MARY) Leave it. We'll want it later...

JOYCE: (*Over this*) Oh, Mary, I almost forgot... Here... (*Out of her pocket, a small booklet*) This is for you... A present.

MARY: *(Wiping her hands on her apron)* What—? What is it? *('smiles')* A present for me?

GEORGE: It cost like two dollars.

HANNAH: George…

GEORGE: *(A joke)* We all chipped in.

(Hands her the booklet)

JOYCE: Read it. Read the title.

MARY: *(Reads)* Cookies for Eleanor. *(Shows it)*

JOYCE: They had a pile of them at the Val Kill gift shop.

MARY: I didn't know Eleanor made cookies.

JOYCE: I don't think she did. I think those are the cookies she just liked to eat.

GEORGE: *(Standing)* Joyce… Mom sees *me* every day.

(JOYCE takes one last "final" sip of coffee:)

JOYCE: Okay. Okay. I'm feeling guilty. I'm ready… Oh give me strength… *(She stands.)*

KARIN: Patricia said she wanted a cup of tea…

GEORGE: *(For the thousandth time)* Our mother, Karin, never says what she means…

JOYCE: No, she doesn't… *(To HANNAH)* Come on, you're coming too…

HANNAH: Daughters-in-law *(Looks at MARY)* have been excused.

JOYCE: Who the hell excused you?

HANNAH: I think—*we* did. *(To MARY)* Didn't we?

MARY: I think so.

HANNAH: *(To KARIN)* Even *ex*-daughters-in-law, Karin. Stay with us… Stay in here… You won't regret it…

JOYCE: *(As she goes with GEORGE)* That doesn't seem fair.

HANNAH: *(Calls)* It does to us!

(They are gone.)

HANNAH: *(To* KARIN*)* You don't want to be in there…

MARY: No. And we speak from experience…

(Laughter)

HANNAH: *(To* MARY*)* What are you making for dinner?

KARIN: I probably shouldn't stay…I don't know…

(Then)

MARY: *(To* HANNAH*)* I was thinking— Ratatouille…
That's easy enough. With—pasta…

(Lights fade.)

2.
Three Sisters-in-law

(A short time later)

*(Off, from the living room, someone is playing the
piano: Schumann's Album for the Youth [no. 6 Armes
Waisenkind].)*

*(*KARIN *still sits on the bench with the cookbooks;* HANNAH
and MARY *at the table, in the middle of a conversation:)*

HANNAH: They've rented out all of Wilderstein.

MARY: How much does that cost?

HANNAH: *(Explains everything:)* Rich people.

MARY: Hannah works for a caterer in Rhinebeck, Karin.

HANNAH: When there's work. *(Like this:)* Weddings…

KARIN: *(Over this)* What's Wilderstein?

HANNAH: A big old beautiful mansion. A park now.
In Rhinebeck. A lot of people here have worked really
hard to restore it. A lot of local history there. Mary,

my boss said she heard they first tried to rent out the
Roosevelt home. They said they really wanted a party
in there. Mary, what can I do?

KARIN: How can I help? I think it'll be fine…I think I
can do what I was going to do—later. Tomorrow even.
I just can't stay too late. When do you think you'll eat?

MARY: *(After a look at* HANNAH*)* An hour and…a half?
Something like that. Is that too late?

KARIN: No. No, that'd be fine. Perfect even.

MARY: Good. Good.

KARIN: So what can I do? And it's all right? You're
sure?

MARY: Of course. You'll need an apron. Hannah, she'll
need an apron. *(To* KARIN*)* You don't want to stain that
lovely blouse…

(HANNAH *finds an apron in the cupboard.*)

MARY: And we'll get you things to cut up…

KARIN: I think I overdressed. I thought maybe there'd
be more of a—ceremony? I guess. But it was perfect.
And I'd never been to something like that before.
Hannah, thank you for the boots. I left them in the
mudroom…

(HANNAH *gives her an apron, as she puts it on, notices the
design:*)

KARIN: I like this… *(Smiles, continues)* I hadn't
realized—what a dope I am—that it'd be a real walk
to the water. I don't know what I'd have done without
those boots.

HANNAH: Well we had to get to the water. That was
sort of the whole point, *(To* MARY*)* wasn't it? What he
wanted… *(To* MARY*)* Thomas loved that river…

KARIN: Thank you, Mary, for letting me tag along. It meant a lot...

MARY: *(Looking in the refrigerator)* So what needs to be cut up...? *(She closes the refrigerator.)* Karin, I keep the [a list:] mushrooms, onions... in the mudroom. *(To* HANNAH*)* I just started doing that.

HANNAH: It's cool out there... I should do that.

MARY: The refrigerator was getting too crowded.

HANNAH: Mine's a mess...

MARY: *(To* KARIN*)* Would you mind? Bring just what you can carry. That should be enough. They're in little baskets...

*(*KARIN *starts to go off.)*

MARY: *(Calls to* KARIN*)* Also tomatoes! Three or four tomatoes!

*(*KARIN *is off.)*

MARY: *(To* HANNAH*)* God only knows how good they are this time of year. Or where they come from...

*(*HANNAH *looks at her.)*

MARY: *(Before* HANNAH *can say anything)* We have enough food... It's fine.

HANNAH: *(To* MARY*)* Joyce said it was snowing in the city when she left this morning.

MARY: We got nothing up here. What a crazy winter.

HANNAH: *(Putting on her apron)* That's not my husband playing.

MARY: You can tell that? That it's Joyce?

HANNAH: Patricia's making her play.

MARY: Does she really need to be made? She never seemed to need...

*(*GEORGE *enters.)*

HANNAH: See?

GEORGE: See what?

HANNAH: That it's your sister playing the piano.

GEORGE: I'm sure I'm next... Has Karin gone?

HANNAH: In the mudroom.

GEORGE: Mom wants her little sherry glass; she says you're always hiding it, Mary.

MARY: I *wash* it. I put it away. In the dining room.

(GEORGE *heads to the dining room.*)

MARY: There were two. She took one to the home. Top shelf, corner cabinet.

(GEORGE *is off.*)

MARY: (*The obvious place:*) It's with the sherry...

HANNAH: Patricia's got her kids waiting on her. That always makes her happy...

MARY: (*Back with the coffeepot*) Do I make coffee or not?

HANNAH: (*Looking at her watch*) Who's going to drink it?

(MARY *will put the coffee back in the refrigerator, and the water pitcher.*)

MARY: (*Back to* HANNAH'*s story*) So all of Wilderstein...? How rich is the guy? And who has their wedding in early March? There are other aprons...

HANNAH: (*About the apron*) This is fine. (*Continues*) I saw... Two tents. A truck just to heat the tents. All of us were guessing it must be like *his* fifth wedding.

MARY: Worse than Thomas. What are you serving? At this—fancy wedding?

(HANNAH *will get plates, cutting boards, knives, etc. in preparation for cutting and slicing the vegetables, as:*)

HANNAH: They're New Yorkers, so they have their own caterer. Their own *New York food*. We just serve it. *(Suddenly to* MARY*)* Oh I saw their chef! He was wearing jeans and cowboy boots. It's fucking Dutchess County not Deadwood. New Yorkers…

*(*GEORGE *returns with a sherry bottle and the special sherry glass. off,* JOYCE *has changed to a faster piece from the Schumann: no. #8: Wilder Reiter.)*

GEORGE: *(About the piano music)* Joyce is showing off now… *(To* HANNAH*)* She said she hadn't touched a piano in six months… Right, Joyce. Right.

*(*KARIN *has returned with some vegetables.)*

*(*GEORGE *looks at* HANNAH*.)*

HANNAH: *(Explaining)* Karin can stay for dinner.

GEORGE: Good. Good. The more the merrier. *(Smiles at* KARIN *and he goes off.)*

KARIN: *(About the vegetables)* How's this? This enough?

MARY: How many of us are we—now? *(To herself)* It keeps growing… *(To* HANNAH*)* You think Patricia is going to eat?

*(*HANNAH *takes the vegetables and will go to the sink, to wash and clean the mushrooms and tomatoes.)*

KARIN: Mary, why all the apples out there…? You must have like a bushel—

MARY: I was all set to make my apple crisp. Then Joyce phoned up— *(In* JOYCE*'s voice)* "I think we should have a cake. Treat the day like his birthday or something". It's not Thomas' birthday. It's sort of the opposite… *("Smiles", then to* HANNAH*)* Joyce says "I'll pay for the cake".

HANNAH: Has she? Paid for the cake?

*(*MARY *looks at her: of course not.)*

MARY: Sit down. Sit, Karin...

HANNAH: *(At the sink washing vegetables)* You can still make your apple crisp... Come on. *(The tomatoes)* These look pretty good. *(Incredulous)* Stop 'n Shop??

MARY: *(No:)* Adams. *(To* KARIN*)* Kingston.

HANNAH: Mary's apple crisp, Karin, was always Thomas' favorite dessert. I can tell her that right?

KARIN: I didn't know that.... I never made him—

HANNAH: *Mary's* apple crisp. Only hers.

KARIN: Of course.

*(*MARY *takes out vegetables for the ratatoille as:)*

MARY: Talk about rich people, Hannah. When Thomas was rehearsing one of his plays in London, there was this party. *(The connection to* HANNAH*)* Rich people. I just remembered this the other day. I keep remembering his stories.

HANNAH: Of course you do. That's normal.

MARY: *(Continues)* And this party was hosted by the Lord Mayor of London. For the theater company that was going to do Thomas' play. *(She moves the trash can to the table.)* We can put the peelings in here.

KARIN: You don't compost? I thought everyone in the country—

MARY: We don't. *(Continues, and continues to set up)* And so Thomas went to this party; it was a fundraiser, in the theater's lobby after a show. And the Lord Mayor, Thomas said was drunk, and had a funny chain kind of thing across his chest... Thomas wrote me about it. I came across the letter last week... I've been re-reading a lot of his letters... *(Then, continues:)* So the people in charge of this party—get this—they had asked the theater company to have some of the younger, by which I'm sure they meant sexier—

HANNAH: Right.

MARY: *(Over this)* —maybe they even came out and said that—members of the acting company—actresses—

HANNAH: Of course.

MARY:—if they could wear the costumes from the show they had been doing that night at this party for potential patrons… Ask me what the show was.

KARIN: What was the show?

MARY: *The Beggar's Opera.*

(They laugh.)

MARY: *(Saying it yet another way)* Rich people… Another planet. A whole other universe.

(Off, the same fast Schumann [no. #8: Wilder Reiter] is being played much faster, and with more bravado:)

HANNAH: Now *that's* George.

(They are listening)

HANNAH: He too has been practicing. He knew they'd both be asked to play…

(HANNAH will join KARIN at the table; MARY continues to set up, clean up, etc.)

KARIN: How thin do you want me to… [cut these]?

MARY: Whatever. I usually…

KARIN: What? Tell me.

MARY: Any way—

HANNAH: Tell her. She wants to do it as *you'd* like.

KARIN: I'll do it any way you want, Mary.

MARY: Quarter inch…?

KARIN: Quarter inch it is.

(HANNAH cuts:)

HANNAH: Like that, Mary?

(MARY *nods.*)

HANNAH: *(To* KARIN*)* Like that. *(To* MARY*)* Was that so hard?

MARY: *(Continues her story)* Some actors did wear their costumes at this party. He wrote all about this in the letter. I just read it again last week.

HANNAH: You said.

MARY: Did I? *(Continues)* So they came in these 19th century beggar clothes, their faces dirtied… And all these drunks from the City just looking down the girl's dresses…

HANNAH: Grow up, men… My boss introduced me to the client, "the groom."

(Off, a telephone rings. HANNAH *starts to get up, he piano playing stops, and then the ringing stops:)*

HANNAH: George got it. *(Continues)* She told him I'd worked "Chelsea's wedding". He was so impressed.

KARIN: Did you really?

HANNAH: I just served—

KARIN: Still…

MARY: *(Over this)* Of course, that type would be…

HANNAH: He *had* to know what wines *Chelsea* served.

KARIN: What were they?

HANNAH: There's a winery in Clinton Corners. The *Clinton* Winery. Their wine. Chelsea must have thought it was cute…

MARY: *(To* KARIN*)* Clinton Corners it's just…

HANNAH: *(Over this)* So this client says: do you think it's too late to get our wine from them too? I don't know what that conjured up... *(Explains everything) The Clintons...!*

MARY: "I want what they want..."

HANNAH: *(Over the end of this)* I get him to order *thirty* cases. Called my friend out in Clinton Corners and told her to charge the fools three times what they usually get.

MARY: Good. Good.

KARIN: And that's what they paid?

HANNAH: *(Explaining)* New Yorkers, Karin, don't know what anything is worth anymore...

(GEORGE enters.)

GEORGE: Your daughter's on the phone, Mary.

(MARY quickly wipes her hands:)

MARY: *(With a "smile")* She called... *(And begins to hurry off.)*

HANNAH: *(To MARY)* Give her our love.

MARY: I will.

GEORGE: I did.

(MARY heads off.)

HANNAH: *(Calls after her)* Tell her we missed her today... But that we understand...

(MARY is gone.)

HANNAH: *(To GEORGE)* She called...

(GEORGE nods.)

GEORGE: *(Looks at the table)* We just had lunch.

HANNAH: *(As joke)* So you're not going to get hungry? Ratatouille. I think Mary's going to make Thomas' apple crisp...

GEORGE: Good...

KARIN: That was one of Thomas' favorites. I just learned that.

GEORGE: I know.

KARIN: From an earlier marriage? Her daughter? I didn't know Mary had a daughter...

GEORGE: *(Nods)* Yeh... An earlier marriage...

HANNAH: *(To KARIN)* She lives in Pittsburgh...

(Off piano music has begun again: another from the Schumann, though slower: no. 9 Volksliedchen.*)*

GEORGE: Joyce told Mom she hadn't touched a piano in about six months... *(Laughs to himself. He will sit and pick up the* Cookies For Eleanor *booklet.)*

HANNAH: Did Patricia criticize Joyce's playing?

(No response)

HANNAH: What did she say? I don't think your mother hears herself sometimes.

(Seeing MARY returning)

HANNAH: That was quick.

MARY: She's busy. She's going to send an e-card... *("Smiles")* I told her she didn't have to do that.

HANNAH: There are a lot of great e-cards now. What's her name, Jackie...something?

(MARY turns on the water.)

KARIN: *(About her cutting)* How am I doing?

HANNAH: *(Looks)* Good... That knife okay?

KARIN: It's fine.

MARY: I'm glad she thought of calling. She's so busy. Nice to hear her voice... *(To GEORGE)* You're not going to be missed?

GEORGE: In there? *(Living room. Shrugs, as: reads the title of the booklet, he's been looking at)* "Cookies for Eleanor."

HANNAH: *(Amazed)* A cookbook about what Eleanor Roosevelt just liked to eat… *(Looks up, to* MARY*)* Mary, they had a neat display—of everything out of Eleanor's purse from, I think, the 1950s? *(To* GEORGE*)* Or maybe it was when she died?

GEORGE: I don't know. It's a clever idea. "Inside the woman's purse…"

HANNAH: *(To* GEORGE*)* Don't say anything you'll regret. *(To* MARY*)* Nail scissors. Makeup. Eleanor's handgun license. Who knew Eleanor Roosevelt packed heat?

MARY: *(Over this)* She had a gun license?? *(She will go to the sink to wash things.)*

HANNAH: *(To* MARY*)* Did you tell her about finding the hair? You wanted to tell your daughter about that.

MARY: She was rushing off somewhere.

HANNAH: *(To* MARY*)* She has a baby…I remember when I had Paulie, I couldn't think about anything else. I missed birthdays… Young mothers…

*(*GEORGE *and* KARIN *are confused. then:)*

GEORGE: *(To* HANNAH*)* What hair? I don't think I know about this…

HANNAH: Should I tell him? *(Then:)* Mary found one of Thomas' grey hairs inside a book. One of those? On the bench there? She was trying to go through his boxes. *(To* GEORGE*)* What do you do with something like that? A hair…

GEORGE: What do you mean?

HANNAH: Mary told me she almost threw it into the wastebasket. Then thought better of that and set the hair aside—on the top of some unopened box? *(After*

a look at MARY:*)* Then... ? She got a phone call or
something...?

*(*MARY *works.)*

HANNAH: Maybe went to the bathroom? Anyway,
Mary comes back and opens up a few more boxes and
about an hour later she remembers the hair. She looks
all around and she can't find it anywhere. She opens
the books... She tells herself—it's just a hair... "Why
am I crying about a hair?"

*(*GEORGE *looks to* HANNAH: *"She was crying?")*

HANNAH: But there's a happy ending, right? When
she's getting ready for bed, on the shoulder of her
sweater—the hair. Now she's scotch-taped it to an
index card and she keeps it in her purse. It's in your
purse?

*(*MARY *nods.)*

*(*HANNAH *goes to* MARY's *purse hanging on a chair by the
desk.)*

GEORGE: *(Trying to be light)* A woman's purse.

(Piano music has stopped off.)

MARY: *(Listens, to* GEORGE*)* Sounds like your sister has
stopped entertaining your mother.

HANNAH: I'm not sure that's something she knows
how to stop doing. Here it is.

*(*HANNAH *the index card to* GEORGE. *He looks at it.)*

KARIN: May I see it? *(She reaches for the index card.)*
Thomas' hair...

MARY: *(Watching her)* It doesn't smell.

*(*JOYCE *enters startling them.)*

JOYCE: *(Entering, to* GEORGE*)* Where did you go?! The
phone rings and you run away... *Your turn.*

(KARIN *smells the hair on the index card.*)

JOYCE: *(Confused)* What are you doing?

HANNAH: Making ratatouille...

(HANNAH *takes the index card from* KARIN *and will hand it back to* MARY.)

GEORGE: *(Standing, to* JOYCE*)* So where is she? Where's Mom now...?

JOYCE: Still in her chair. No doubt still criticizing me.

GEORGE: Joyce, she hasn't been criticizing... *(He heads off.)*

JOYCE: *(Over this, as her mother, to* GEORGE*)* "Is that how you're going to play it? Is that how you're going to play it?"

GEORGE: *(Calls, over this)* Grow up, Joyce... *(He is gone.)*

JOYCE: *(To "*GEORGE*")* Fuck you.

MARY: I thought you sounded great, Joyce...

JOYCE: I've been practicing. Don't tell my brother. *(She smiles at* KARIN.)

HANNAH: Karin is staying for dinner...

JOYCE: *(Taken aback)* Good...

(MARY *has taken the index card to her purse.*)

JOYCE: What's that?

HANNAH: One of Thomas' hairs. Mary keeps it taped to an index card, in her purse...

JOYCE: Why???

MARY: *(Changing the subject)* I know your mother really appreciates your coming up today, Joyce.

JOYCE: Has she said that? Has she actually said that?

MARY: I think so...

(Then:)

(Lights fade.)

3.
Common Sense in the Kitchen

(The same. A short time later. Off, Satie's piano solo, 3 Grossiennes.)

(HANNAH and KARIN sit at the table slicing vegetables for the ratatouille. MARY hovers, cleaning up, getting things ready... JOYCE sits, looking through an old cookbook that she has found lying on the table.)

(In the middle of conversation:)

JOYCE: *(Reading from the old book in hand)* "Tell me, dear reader, do you often say to yourself, in bitterness of spirit, that it is a mistake to educate girls into a love of science and literature, and then condemn them to the routine of a domestic drudge."

KARIN: *(To MARY)* When was this was written?

JOYCE: "1884."

KARIN: *(To JOYCE)* And it's a woman?

HANNAH: Has to be a woman...

JOYCE: *(Reads the cover)* "Marion Harland." A woman.

KARIN: I think I'm cutting these too thick.

HANNAH: That's fine... You're doing great...

MARY: *(About the music)* This was one of Thomas' favorites...

JOYCE: That's what she wants. That's what Mom's asking for. Pieces Thomas used to play for her...
(Reads) "A talk, as woman to woman." *(The point is proved)* Woman to woman... There you go. "An informal preface to what I mean shall be an informal book..." A woman talking to women, who's listened

to other women… *(Just remembers a "story")* Hannah, I
heard a joke this week—. A girl tells her Mother about
her new boyfriend… Her Mom asks what he does.
The mom is shocked: "How can you go out with *him?*
Someone who works for the N S A!" The daughter just
looks at her mother, her eyes wide open, "But Mom—
he listens."

(They laugh.)

JOYCE: A friend told me that. A married friend…

HANNAH: Keep reading… *(To* MARY*)* I don't think we
read this part.

JOYCE: *(Reads)* "My dear fellow-housekeeper and
reader."

HANNAH: That's us…

JOYCE: "I have before me now a picture of a wife and
mother, in slatternly morning-gown at four in the
afternoon, leaning back in the laziest and most ragged
of rocking-chairs, dust on the carpet, on the *open*
piano—" I love that touch—her "reader" is all alone at
home, playing her piano. *(Then)* I've been there. Who
hasn't been there?

(MARY now joins them at the table.)

JOYCE: *(Continues to read)* "…dust on the mantel, the
mirrors, even on her own hair, she rubs the soft palm
of one hand with the grimy fingers of the other, and
with a sickly-sweet smile whines out: "I have no talent
for housework". *(Looks up, to* MARY, *about the book)*
These were all Thomas's?

(MARY nods.)

HANNAH: We were surprised too.

KARIN: Research for something.

MARY: I don't know what. That whole pile there. I
thought they belonged in the kitchen.

HANNAH: She found them in a plastic box in his office…

JOYCE: *(As she looks at the pile of books)* All of them about cooking? Why would my brother—?

KARIN: Did he start cooking? Thomas never cooked when we were married.

MARY: No. He couldn't cook anything. *(She cuts onions.)*

JOYCE: That's what I— [thought].

MARY: *(Over this)* Maybe pasta. Maybe. That's what he always *said* he could cook. If I hadn't made anything, if I was busy— *(In Thomas' voice)* "I can cook pasta."

HANNAH: Did he mean it?

MARY: I don't know. I don't know.

KARIN: You should have—

MARY: Tested him? I know. I know.

JOYCE: That would have been fun.

MARY: It would have been.

(MARY wipes her eyes. HANNAH looks at her.)

MARY: The onions, Hannah.

HANNAH: *(To JOYCE)* He's written notes, quotes from things in the backs of some of them.

JOYCE: Thomas?

HANNAH: In the margins. Thumb through. *(Reaching for a book:)* One—something about: how it is the one thing everyone lies about…I think it's this one.

KARIN: What is?

MARY: What you eat—when you're alone…

HANNAH: *(With the book)* Yes. Here… That's what he wrote… *(Reads)* "Everyone lies about what they eat when they're alone." *(As she shows* KARIN*)* Do you lie about that? What you eat when you're alone?

(No response)

HANNAH: I lie about that.

(JOYCE *continues to read to herself.)*

HANNAH: And here...Mary thinks he just jotted down things he'd find... Something he'd heard or read and just remembered: here: "human beings are the only animals that transform their food. That *cook."*

MARY: He underlines: "cook".

HANNAH: *(Reads)* "So it is one of the things that makes us human beings..."

KARIN: *(As she cuts)* Some birds—don't they regurgitate what they eat—for their babies?

MARY: That's not cooking.

KARIN: I guess not.

JOYCE: *(Looking at the book)* You haven't tried *my* cooking.

HANNAH: The first time George wanted to cook for me... He forgot to wash the lettuce. So you could— hear—the crunch of the dirt, as you ate. Like little bits of gravel. I didn't say anything.

JOYCE: You think he even noticed? I know my brother.

HANNAH: The next night *I* offered to wash the lettuce.

KARIN: That was a nice way to handle that... Very generous...

HANNAH: I thought so.

KARIN: *(Cutting)* I don't think I'm that generous...

JOYCE: Listen to this: "When *I* took possession—

HANNAH: Thomas?

JOYCE: No, "Marion Harland". "When *I* took possession of *my* first real home the prettily furnished cottage to which I came as a bride, so full of hope and courage; after one day's investigation I knew my lately-hired servants –" *(Looks up)* She had servants…"…knew no more about cookery than I did, or perhaps affected stupidity to determine my capabilities."

HANNAH: Sounds like a nightmare… *(To* KARIN*)* That's why I don't have servants.

JOYCE: "And I was too proud to let them suspect the truth, I shut myself up with my *Complete Housewives. I guess* that's some book. *(Looks at the cover)* It's not this book. *(Reads)* "I do not like to remember that time!"

HANNAH: Poor thing.

JOYCE: *(Over this, reads)* "My wrestling begat nothing but pitiable confusion, hopeless distress, and a three-days' sick headache, during which season I am not sure that I did not darkly contemplate suicide… *(Looks up, then continues)* …as the only sure escape from the meshes that strangle me."

MARY: I didn't read that far… God.

KARIN: This is Marion—?

JOYCE: The author. *(Showing her)* It's the introduction: "Familiar talk with my reader."

MARY: I mostly just looked at the recipes. And his notes…

(As they chop, peel:)

JOYCE: *(Reads)* "At the height or depth of my despondency a friend, one with a great heart and steady brain, came to my rescue."

KARIN: How—?

HANNAH: Sh-sh.

JOYCE: "Her cheerful laugh over my dilemma rings down to me now, through all these years. "Bless your innocent little heart!" she cried, "Ninety-nine out of a hundred cookbooks are written by people who never kept house, and the hundredth by a good cook who doesn't know how to express herself. Rule Number One: Compile a recipe book for yourself. And take your time. Learn one thing at a time, and when you have mastered it, make a note on it, never losing sight of this principle—you only learn, by doing." *(Looks up)* Why wasn't *she* my mother?

MARY: There's nothing wrong with your mother.

(JOYCE looks at the book, then looks up.)

JOYCE: When I was like thirteen or something… *(To* HANNAH*)* Did I ever tell you this?

HANNAH: Joyce, I don't know what you're going to—

JOYCE: It's Christmas morning—and I unwrap—the fucking *Joy Of Cooking.* "That's all you need, dear heart" Mom says to me, smiling her smile. "All you need in life." Thanks, Mom. Thank you very much. A really big help. I'm ready for life now! Bring it on!

KARIN: Wasn't she just trying to—?

JOYCE: I know. I know.

HANNAH: *(To* KARIN*)* Let her—

JOYCE: "Let her" what?

KARIN: I like the *Joy Of Cooking.*

HANNAH: *(To* MARY*)* I know what she means.

JOYCE: *(To* HANNAH*)* As if it were the gift of life. And the way she— "hands" it over, Hannah. *(Gestures)* Like passing some torch. Or an heirloom. My dowry.

MARY: Was it *her* copy?

JOYCE: No. No. Brand fucking new. Like she was giving me the god damn *Joy Of Sex*.

(The piano music off has stopped by now. They listen for a moment:)

JOYCE: He stopped...

HANNAH: Actually my Mom gave me—

KARIN: She didn't. No.

HANNAH: *(Over the end of this) The Joy Of Sex.* She sort of did. Left her and Dad's copy lying around.

JOYCE: On purpose?

HANNAH: *(Shrugs)* That's what I think now.

JOYCE: At least she didn't "hand" it to you. *(Turns back to* MARY*)* Like she was giving me something incredibly "valuable". A "mother-daughter event". I don't think I even opened it up.

MARY: That must have hurt her.

JOYCE: *(Shrugs)* I was thirteen... She should have known better.

KARIN: I agree. *(Remembering her thirteenth year) Thirteen*...I hated that age. My skin was like...

JOYCE: Another time—I was I think almost seventeen. Trying like hell to get out of here.

KARIN: *(As she cuts) Seventeen* wasn't much better...

JOYCE: *(Over this)* I come into here, this very kitchen –

MARY: *(To* KARIN*)* I thought you and Thomas got married when you were like—*nineteen*...

KARIN: Those are two completely different universes: seventeen and nineteen. They were for me. Completely and totally different—planets.

(They let that sink in, then:)

JOYCE: *(Starts again)* I come into this very kitchen, and there's Mom, right there [points] where you are, Karin, she holds a bowl. *(Mimes: stirring)* Mixing something. She looks like a witch mixing a potion.

MARY: I like your Mom. I like her a lot.

JOYCE: I like her too, for Christ sake. I'm telling a story. Let me tell my story.

HANNAH: And so what happened?

JOYCE: She looks up at me from her "stirring", gets that "look". We all know that look.

KARIN: *(To* HANNAH*)* What's the look—?

JOYCE: *(Same time)* "What's wrong, Mom?" I say. I *think* I sounded concerned. I tried. I remember trying. *(Mother's voice)* "I'm making my birthday cake, dear heart." It was the "dear heart".

MARY: That's cute.

JOYCE: She's not your mother.

KARIN: *(To* HANNAH*)* Her *own* cake. You can't win that...

JOYCE: It was her birthday. "Come on, Mom", I say in my most "perky" way, "I really don't think *you* should be making your own birthday cake, on your own birthday".

HANNAH: You actually said that? *(Incredulous)* You know you walked right into it.

KARIN: *(What could she do:)* She's seventeen.

JOYCE: "Then who's going to make it?" Mom asks. And suddenly she's not crying anymore but all "bubbly" and smiley and "perky" too.

MARY: *(Critical)* Joyce—

JOYCE: I'm being fair. I'm not being unfair. So I start to see where this is all headed. "Why can't we just buy a cake, Mom? I'll go to that bakery in Kingston you like so much. O K?" She stops being bubbly and smiley and perky. I stand right about where you were Hannah. By your chair. My brothers both sit here. Maybe *they* will make it?

(No response)

MARY: *(Matter of fact)* So you make your mother a cake. Good for you.

KARIN: I have two brothers. I'm with you.

JOYCE: I make her the goddamn birthday cake. And as I get going I start convincing myself that this is really a special what—honor? My chance to shine maybe? To show up my brothers? So I really work on that damn cake. Right at this table. Here. I work really really *really* hard on it. And when I "present" my cake? When she sees my great effort, when I am finally done? And push the sweaty hair out of my eyes? Wipe the sweat off my god damn zitty face? Mom says, "dear heart, you worked so hard".

(This sinks in, then:)

KARIN: Oh boy…

MARY: I know what she *meant*.

JOYCE: It's not how *she* would have made it.

KARIN: "Dear heart" *is* cute. It's old fashioned.

MARY: *(Over this)* That's not what she said, Joyce. She didn't say that.

KARIN: *(Over this)* That's what she heard.

JOYCE: Thank you, Karin.

(Pause as they chop and cut.)

HANNAH: *(Hinting, to* JOYCE*)* The cake *you* asked Mary to buy for today was store bought…

JOYCE: From Deising's? You got it at Deising's…?

MARY: It's from Deising's.

JOYCE: Thomas always loved their cakes. Least I
thought of that... At least I did something right
today... *(Reads from the book again)* Should I keep
reading?

THE OTHERS: Yes. Yes.

JOYCE: *(Reads)* "And these notes were the first of
practical wisdom and receipts I now offer for your
inspection." *(She holds up the book.)* She calls recipes
"receipts". "Never forget that you are mistress of
yourself. Have faith in your own abilities. I take it
for granted that you, dear reader, are too intelligent
to share in the vulgar prejudice against labor-saving
machines." *She'd* have a micro-wave... *(Then)* I have a
micro-wave...

KARIN: I couldn't live without my—

JOYCE: Mom knows they don't kill you, right?

MARY: Your mother liked what she had...

JOYCE: You don't have to keep explaining my mother
to me. *(Reads)* "Many excellent—." *(She starts to read,
stops:)* When I told Mom I'd actually bought a micro-
wave for *my* tiny Brooklyn apartment kitchen? It was
like I'd robbed someone or kicked a dog... Or denied
global warming. "Mom, I didn't do anything wrong."
"It's wrong." Not in this century. Or the last one...
(Continues to read) "...Many excellent housewives have
a fashion of saying loftily, "I carry all my receipts" —
recipes— "in my head. I never wrote out one in my life.
And so you, if timid and self-distrustful, are smitten
with shame—"

HANNAH: I have an aunt who says that. She says it's all
in her head. My Mom's little sister. My Mom told me
not to believe anything she said.

JOYCE: *(Continues over this, reads)* "My advice is—just keep your recipe-book out of sight." Like a battle. She's preparing us, suiting us up, for some battle... So we're not what? Intimidated?

HANNAH: Times have changed. Thank god. Haven't they?

MARY: *(As she cuts)* Thomas has—had—these friends –

KARIN: Who—?

MARY: He met them with me, later; so you probably wouldn't know them. You go to their apartment—first it's always incredibly neat.

HANNAH: *(Obvious)* Then they have a cleaner.

KARIN: I'm sure you're right.

MARY: *(Over this)* The kitchen—a kind of stove that just— *(Makes the point)* intimidates.

HANNAH: I hate those. I really hate those.

MARY: She cooks while she talks. She can do that. While she sips wine and cooks, she tells funny and often self-deprecating stories. How does she do that? Doesn't she have to fucking *measure*? She cleans pots *while* she's cooking *and* telling the stories *and* drinking the goddamn wonderful wine, and almost every time she's in her goddamn bare feet. I hated going there for dinner.

HANNAH: It's the bare feet that takes it over the edge.

JOYCE: *(Continues to read)* "Here I lay down a few safe and imperative rules for your kitchen –" *(Dramatic pause, others look up)* "— never stand when you can do your work as well while sitting."

(They are all sitting.)

HANNAH: We do *that*. We're good at that.

MARY: We are. *(Makes a check mark)* Check.

JOYCE: "It will sometimes happen that when you have heated your pitch—"

KARIN: What does that mean?

JOYCE: —"swabbed your deck, or made your pudding, the result is—failure. No part of your culinary education is more useful; you have learned how not to do it right, which is the next thing to success." I guess I'm closer to success than I thought. "However, should any such mishaps occur, do not vex or amuse your husband and your guests with the narration…" In other words, don't tell them…

HANNAH: I'm interested in this.

JOYCE: *(Reads)* "…with the narration, still less with visible proof of the calamity." So hide it. "Many a partial failure would pass unobserved but for the clouded brow and earnest apologies of the hostess."

HANNAH: This is about a lot more than cooking.

JOYCE: "Do not apologize!" Exclamation mark. *(Shows them, and reads)* "You will be astonished to find, if you keep your wits about you, how often even your husband will remain in blissful ignorance that nothing has gone wrong, *if* you do not tell him."

HANNAH: "Do not tell him…" Have any of you ever done that? Ever happen to you?

(Heads down, they chop.)

HANNAH: I've done that. I'll bet we've all done that. And now we know there's nothing wrong in doing that…. Let me see that book.

(JOYCE hands HANNAH the book. HANNAH wipes her hands:)

JOYCE: It has someone's recipes—

HANNAH: "Receipts."

JOYCE: She's pinned them in—with little pins. Like keepsakes.

KARIN: That's sweet.

HANNAH: *(Reads the title page)* "Common Sense in the Household. A Manual of Practical Housewifery." 1884. *(Shows the title page) This* sat in someone's kitchen for years and years.

MARY: Maybe generations.

KARIN: The family cookbook.

MARY: Like the family bible. Maybe more revealing. *(Explains)* What goes on in the kitchen...

HANNAH: This is Thomas' handwriting... *(Reads)* "The discovery of a new dish does more for mankind than the discovery of a new star."

(MARY will get bowls from the cupboard to collect all the vegetables.)

This is written by someone else, Mary. Maybe the person who gave the woman the book... It's old fashioned handwriting. "Improve each shining hour."

MARY: So he was going to write a story about cooking... Or a play...

HANNAH: *(Reads)* "Never try experiments" —more advice. "— when you have invited guests for dinner. Never risk the success of your meal on a new dish. So introduce your experiments cautiously to your husband, as by-play."

JOYCE: "By-play..."? It says that? "By-play?"

HANNAH: "And never be too *shy* of innovations... Variety can be not only pleasant, but healthy. The pampered palate will soon grow weary of the same bill of fare." This *is* about a lot more than cooking... *(Sees* GEORGE*)*

(GEORGE *enters.*)

GEORGE: Is there any wine, Mary? I'd love a glass of wine...

MARY: There's a half a bottle. On the door. Smell it first...

(GEORGE *goes to the refrigerator;* MARY *will bring him a glass.*)

GEORGE: Mom's asleep. She fell asleep in her chair. *(Before* JOYCE *can say anything)* I couldn't get her to go upstairs, Joyce. I tried. *(Smells the wine)* It's fine. *(Takes the glass)* Thanks. Anyone else?

("No", "Maybe later": no one wants wine now.)

GEORGE: She—insisted on looking through a couple of photo albums. There's the one just of Thomas...

MARY: I keep that album out...

HANNAH: *(To* MARY*)* Long day for her...

GEORGE: *(To* HANNAH*)* She was crying...

HANNAH: I thought your Mom did great this morning. *(To* MARY*)* When you asked if she wanted to help you "scoop" out any of the ashes...I thought—she was going to lose it then...

GEORGE: It's good Mom's asleep... She needs that.

(Lights fade.)

4.
Patricia Gabriel

(The same, a short time later.)

*(*MARY *is at the sink;* HANNAH, JOYCE, KARIN *still at the table, chopping, cutting, peeling.* GEORGE *sits, drinking his wine.)*

(In the middle of conversation:)

HANNAH: These two big guys knock on your Mom's door—she's alone.

MARY: *(Over the end of this)* I was out at the store. If I'd been here...

HANNAH: It's not your fault.

(Timer goes off.)

HANNAH: She thinks it's her fault.

MARY: I should have been here.

HANNAH: Come on...

HANNAH: And these guys tell your mother—. *(To GEORGE)* Right? *(To JOYCE)* They're putting down new asphalt on another driveway down the street, and so—

GEORGE: How her driveway looks "dangerous". And a lot of other bullshit.

HANNAH: If someone fell, and so forth. "Lawsuits."

JOYCE: They say that: lawsuits?

GEORGE: To scare you.

HANNAH: "Oh and by the way—"

GEORGE: *(Over the end of this)* "And by the way—"' she's so "lucky" *because* they are right now just down South Street, so that will save Mom a whole lot of money. Normally they wouldn't even be doing this in December. But it's been bizarrely warm...

KARIN: *(To MARY)* Your timer...

HANNAH: They took advantage of an old woman.

JOYCE: Shit. She wrote a check—?

GEORGE: Mom wrote the check. They "needed it right away". They probably ran to the bank to cash it.

HANNAH: By the time Mary is back from the store...

MARY: I'd been gone maybe forty, forty-five minutes, Joyce.

GEORGE: (Over this) They're already pouring the asphalt.

MARY: George thinks it won't last...

GEORGE: It won't. You don't do this kind of job in winter. Even if it's warm for a few days... It's just going to crumble.

HANNAH: Seven thousand four hundred dollars.

JOYCE: Shit. Oh shit...

(Short pause)

(MARY lowers the oven temperature, and resets the timer.)

JOYCE: Does she have that kind of money to just...?

GEORGE: The check didn't bounce. We were hoping it would bounce...

(MARY takes out a frying pan; she will go and get oil from the pantry cupboard.)

JOYCE: I didn't know anything about this...

GEORGE: You haven't been here, Joyce.

JOYCE: I have a phone. A whole brand new driveway for seven thousand dollars? I didn't even notice a difference.

GEORGE: Ever since Thomas died, Mom has seemed scared. Something happened...

HANNAH: Even before...

GEORGE: I suppose you always think you're not going to live longer than your kids...

(MARY turns on the stove, she will pour oil into the frying pan and soon collect the vegetables into a bowl.)

KARIN: (To MARY at the stove) You need any help there...?

MARY: Maybe in a minute.

(The others will help collect the vegetables into bowls. No one knows what to say:)

GEORGE: We should thank Mary.

MARY: Why?

HANNAH: Why?

GEORGE: For this morning. It was really nice this morning. I didn't think that would be so nice, *(To HANNAH)* did I?

HANNAH: No…

GEORGE: I was telling Hannah in the car, I now think I want *my* ashes thrown into the Hudson too. *(A joke, to everyone)* No rush. Please! *(Laughs)* Though maybe next time we can pick a season, Joyce, when we don't have to chop away at the goddamn ice…

HANNAH: There was no ice, George.

GEORGE: It was cold. Mom got cold.

MARY: We had thought we were waiting for spring…

GEORGE: *("Serious" and teasing)* But Joyce is "very busy"…. Unlike us "country folk" who have nothing to do…

JOYCE: *(Over this)* It's a business trip.

GEORGE: "To Europe." "Oh Twist my arm."

MARY: Could you watch this for a minute, Karin?

(KARIN goes to stir the vegetables.)

MARY: Who wants to help peel apples? We can use the same knives…I also have peelers… *(To KARIN)*

HANNAH: You've decided to make your apple crisp?

(MARY heads off to the mudroom.)

HANNAH: *(Calls)* I'll get peelers. *(To* GEORGE*)* She's
going to make her apple crisp... *(To* JOYCE*)* That was
Thomas' favorite.

JOYCE: I know.

HANNAH: *(Getting peelers, bowls, etc.)* We can also have
the cake. We can have both...

GEORGE: *(Back to Mom)* Joyce, last month Mom...

HANNAH: Oh God this is embarrassing.

JOYCE: What? Mom what?

GEORGE: *(To* HANNAH*)* You want to tell her? *(To* JOYCE*)*
Last month, Hannah drops by here. Just as Mary
and Mom are hurrying out to the bank. To send how
much—six hundred dollars, right? To our Paulie...

JOYCE: Why? Why did Paulie—? Where was he—?

GEORGE: We thought he was on his senior class trip to
Washington. You tell her. You were here.

*(*HANNAH *wipes her hands then:)*

HANNAH: "There you are", your mother says the
moment I walk in. "We've been trying to call you.
We're on our way to the bank and then to the post
office. Paulie, he's not on his senior class trip, he's in
some trouble in Canada."

JOYCE: Canada? What are you talking about? *(To*
GEORGE*)* What?

*(*MARY *returns with a small bushel of apples, and she hears:)*

HANNAH: Somehow they knew our son—her
grandson— was on a—trip.

MARY: Oh god... You're telling her that.

HANNAH: *(Over)* How did they know?

JOYCE: Who?

MARY: When did I become so stupid?

GEORGE: *(Over this)* I still think it was just a lucky guess.

JOYCE: Who?

HANNAH: Your mother got a phone call: "Your grandson's crossed the border, and bought an expensive computer and now he doesn't have the money to pay the duty". *(Explains)* So the customs people at the border are going to confiscate the new computer Paulie's bought, unless we send right away—six hundred dollars. Mary's saying—as I walk in, Mary is saying "We're sending him the money".

MARY: What the heck was I thinking?

HANNAH: *(Over this)* You were worried about our son.

JOYCE: Paulie had called Mom??

HANNAH: *(Looks at GEORGE)* Sort of.

JOYCE: I don't understand.

HANNAH: And then I think to ask Mary if she had talked to Paulie *herself*. No. No, but your mother has. Patricia says, "And Paulie sounds so upset". So the three of us, we hurry to the bank and take out the money, then to the post office so we can wire a money order. By this time I've called George at the shop, so George tries to call Paulie on *his* cell phone. He leaves a message. Tell her...

GEORGE: And then I call the number—

HANNAH:—in Canada where we're supposed to call after we've sent the money. To tell him it's on its way.

GEORGE: A woman answers. *(Then)* I ask for Paulie. And tell her I'm his father. And then Paulie comes on the line. The connection isn't so great, a lot of static, but I hear him say, "Hi Dad. Hi. I'm okay. I have a cold. Are you sending the money? Please send the money. I need money". When... *(Looks at HANNAH)*

JOYCE: What?

GEORGE: When—*my* cell phone rings. And I pick *that* up, I'm still on the other line, on the land line with Paulie—but on my cell, calling me back—is Paulie. He's in Washington, with his classmates. On his senior class trip.

JOYCE: (*Confused*) I don't understand??

GEORGE: The other—in Canada—was someone else.

HANNAH: Someone who happened to sound like Paulie...

GEORGE: With a cold. And a lot of static...I ask that person: who the hell are you?! He hangs up.

HANNAH: George calls me and we're still in line at the post office. Thank god there was a line. (*Into "the phone"*) "Don't send the money. It's a scam."

GEORGE: It's a "popular" scam, we learned from the State Police. They couldn't do anything. Mom had her picture in the paper—as a volunteer at the library? We figure they saw that. They look for old people. Old people to them are "just fish in a fucking barrel". The cop's words...

HANNAH: When you're scared, you're just vulnerable...

(MARY *brings the apples to the table.*)

MARY: She is. We are...I can do that now, Karin. Thank you.

(KARIN *returns to the table.*)

JOYCE: How's Paulie doing?

GEORGE: He's applied to fourteen colleges. So we're— waiting.

HANNAH: It's like Chinese water torture, isn't it?

GEORGE: *(Nods)* Every day you watch you son ask himself: "So what am I worth?" Parents shouldn't have to witness that...

JOYCE: *(About the apples)* From Adams? These must be from Adams. They look great for this time of year...

MARY: The farmers' market...

GEORGE: *(To* HANNAH*)* We always forget to go there...

JOYCE: The farmer's market?

MARY: It's in the winter now too. In the town hall...

(They take knives, peelers, and sit and peel apples. MARY *has gone back to the stove.)*

HANNAH: You know that guy on the News Hour who does the business?

MARY: Paul-something...what? I forget—

KARIN: I watch him.

HANNAH: *(Over this)* The other day he's interviewing some hedgefund guy who's a little defensive: "Come on, are we really bad guys?" And then the guy tried to explain: "Look at those hyenas and the vultures out there on the savannah.... Come on. Are they *bad* guys? Just because there happens to be a sudden boom in carcasses, is that really their fault? They're just taking advantage of `opportunities'...? They're just hungry..."

(Then)

GEORGE: All of a sudden Mom gets on all these lists. Now that she's in her new place, Mary gets all these phone calls... We had no idea. "I'm calling about your credit card accounts..." No they're not. "It's the I R S." No you're not.

MARY: "Congratulations you've won something or other." No, you haven't. "We've got very important

information about your Medicare coverage." No they
don't.

GEORGE: They want to pick over her fucking bones...
She won't show us her checkbook. We don't know
what she's been doing...

HANNAH: Mary throws away most of the
"solicitations" that come in the mail...

MARY: She still gets her mail here. I take her a few
things, so she doesn't get too suspicious.

JOYCE: You hear about families and their parents—they
fight like hell with their kids about moving into... One
of these place.

KARIN: My father was like that...

HANNAH: She's made it so easy for all of us. Bless her.
Bless her...

GEORGE: She has friends there... People she's known
forever...

KARIN: Good for your Mom. You're lucky.

(As they peel:)

HANNAH: It's a nice place.

GEORGE: Very nice.

HANNAH: I know your mother really wants to show
you her apartment, Joyce.

GEORGE: You should go.

JOYCE: Of course I'm going to go. You don't have to tell
me to go. I'll go after dinner. I'm looking forward to
seeing it. Mom's "new life".

GEORGE: Good.

JOYCE: You don't have to make me. I know I should go.

HANNAH: It's just a room. So be prepared. It's a nice
room. It's not a house...

GEORGE: She took things with her. Her desk. Some rugs. The loveseat from her bedroom. Not much more would fit. She's tried to make it a home. It's just up East Market...

JOYCE: I admit to being very surprised, when you called and told me... I thought you must have somehow made her... *(Then)* She seemed to have an "accident" at the diner? At lunch? Or am I wrong?

(HANNAH looks to GEORGE, then)

MARY: It happens.

HANNAH: We try not to make anything of it. It embarrasses her. It happens...

JOYCE: Maybe she should wear—

MARY: She doesn't like the way she looks in them, Joyce. She says they make her look fat.

JOYCE: Maybe we should insist. For her own—

GEORGE: She *sometimes* wears them. She didn't today, Joyce, because she wanted to look her best.

(MARY will cover the simmering vegetables and join the others at the table.)

JOYCE: Is that Mom's car still out in the drive? I thought we were selling that. When I was here in November, I thought you said you were going to sell that.

(HANNAH looks to GEORGE.)

GEORGE: Not yet...

JOYCE: That's just wasting money. You're still paying insurance, the sticker... What? Mom's not still driving, is she? We talked about this...

GEORGE: She's not *really* driving, Joyce.

HANNAH: She keeps it at the home. She drove here this morning. We'll drive her back tonight. In the dark...

She doesn't drive in the dark. She can't see. We'll take two cars...

JOYCE: George—

GEORGE: Joyce, you're right, *we* agreed. Mom just didn't agree...

JOYCE: What?

GEORGE: She said—no. We thought the place wouldn't allow it. Didn't we? We thought that would settle it. *(Shrugs)* But hey, they do. It's "independent living". They said "that's not our job".

JOYCE: She can barely turn her head. She can't see out the back window.

GEORGE: She can turn her head. *(To* HANNAH*)* Can't she?

(No response)

*(*MARY *goes to check on the vegetables.)*

JOYCE: She's going to kill someone. She's going to run over some kid. You told me you were going to do this... You promised.

HANNAH: Mary tell her, your mother hardly drives anywhere.

MARY: *(Lists)* To the Stop 'n Shop. The library. To here...

JOYCE: There are trucks on Route 9. And school buses...

(Then)

(Lights fade.)

5.
Brigadoon

(The same, a short time later.)

(MARY stirs the vegetables. GEORGE, HANNAH, JOYCE and KARIN sit at the table, and slowly methodically peel apples.)

JOYCE: Mary, do you have any red wine?

MARY: In the mudroom.

(JOYCE gets up.)

I keep the red out there.

JOYCE: Any particular—?

MARY: They're all basically the same, Joyce. Cheap.

(JOYCE is off to the mudroom.)

GEORGE: *(To say something)* Karin, you didn't have to teach today? *(He is about to eat an apple slice.)*

HANNAH: They're for the apple crisp, George...

KARIN: *(Answering)* Not on Fridays. No "theater class" on Fridays. I don't know why.

(MARY will taste the vegetables, add salt and pepper as needed. Soon she will add the tomatoes.)

HANNAH: *(Beginning to slice)* Mary? Quarters, then halves again?

MARY: Sure.

HANNAH: *(To GEORGE)* Quarters, and then halves again.... Do it how she says.

GEORGE: *(Continues to KARIN)* So—long weekends. Not bad.

(JOYCE returns with a bottle of red wine.)

GEORGE: Do you go back to the city?

KARIN: I sublet my apartment.

JOYCE: I'm subletting mine for the three months I'm away. You have to. *(Getting herself a glass out of the dish rack)* Anyone else?

(No one wants wine.)

KARIN: *(Peeling)* I don't know how I had the nerve to say I could teach "playwriting". I can just hear Thomas: "You're teaching playwriting...?"

JOYCE: They're kids. Make it up...

MARY: *(About the glass)* That clean?

JOYCE: It was in the dish rack.

KARIN: *(Continues as she peels)* I had no idea what to expect.

GEORGE: I hope you expected rich kids. Hotchkiss.

HANNAH: *(Explaining to JOYCE)* Some teacher got ill all of a sudden. *(To MARY)* Right? Isn't that what happened? That's what Mary said happened.

KARIN: *(Over the end of this)* Needed a body right away. I am that body. I was free... *(Which means:)* I didn't have a job. Probably the tenth actor they tried...

MARY: Karin's been teaching at a school in New York...

HANNAH: I didn't know that.

JOYCE: So it's not completely—

KARIN: Teaching *acting*. And it's not really a school. I really don't know what I'm doing.

MARY: *(Stirring, adding the tomatoes)* Thomas used to tell *his* students, when he taught...

KARIN: When did Thomas teach? I didn't know he ever—

HANNAH: Oh he hated it. How he hated it.

MARY: The school, not the kids...

KARIN: He always told me he'd never teach...

MARY: He lasted maybe two years...

HANNAH: *(Finishing her apples, to* MARY*)* What about a salad, Mary? Shouldn't we have a salad?

MARY: Look in the fridge. Check the lettuce. It's been there a while... *(About Thomas, to* KARIN*)* Let me get this right. I heard him tell this to a bunch of students when they came to our house in New Haven. *(Trying to get it right)* There are two questions a playwright needs to answer. Two. *(Works to get it right)* "Why did you write it?" And then, "Why should we watch it?" *(Pleased with herself)* That was it... So what does that mean?

JOYCE: Make it personal. And make it matter. I think I understand that.

*(*GEORGE *has picked up the booklet:* Cookies For Eleanor *and begins to thumb through it.)*

MARY: *(As* HANNAH *looks at the lettuce)* How's the lettuce?

HANNAH: I can pull off the brown leaves...

MARY: I don't think that's even washed.

HANNAH: *(Over this)* I'll wash it. And I'll pull off the bad leaves...

MARY: *(Continuing, still stirring)* Oh, and Karin, he had a little sign he'd made for himself. I just remembered this.

(Timer goes off.)

MARY: I keep remembering things. All day... Over his desk. In his office. *(Stirring)* "Don't write words, Thomas. Just try and write people."

JOYCE: *(To* KARIN*)* So tell them that... Whatever that means...

KARIN: *(About the sign)* Actors love hearing that kind of stuff. Thomas loved actors.

MARY: He married one...

(Smiles at KARIN*)*

HANNAH: Mary, your bread.

*(*HANNAH *begins to wash the lettuce in the sink.* MARY *will open the oven.)*

GEORGE: *(Musing on the booklet title)* "Cookies for Eleanor..."

JOYCE: I liked going there today. To Eleanor's house. Let me see.

GEORGE: *(About the bread)* That smells good. I'm getting hungry.

HANNAH: *(About* GEORGE*)* It's a reflex.

JOYCE: *(To* GEORGE*)* Are you done?

GEORGE: I was taking a break...

*(*MARY *takes the bread out of the oven.)*

JOYCE: *(About the booklet)* Just what Eleanor liked to eat... Good for her.

HANNAH: *(At the sink)* Eleanor Roosevelt, I think, was the first woman I ever admired.

MARY: I didn't know that.

HANNAH: *(Washing the lettuce)* I was in, maybe, first grade and we had to draw a picture of someone we admired? Everyone drew their father or grandfather maybe mother. I drew Eleanor Roosevelt. Of course I put her in a wedding dress... *(Laughs. She gets the salad spinner from under the sink as:)*

MARY: Of course...

JOYCE: Women come from all over.

GEORGE: You mean to Val Kill?

KARIN: I know women, in the theater, who have come up just to Hyde Park just to see Eleanor's house.

JOYCE: I'm not surprised...

KARIN: There's the little wooden bridge—

HANNAH: We saw that today.

KARIN: —did the guard tell you anything about this bridge?

JOYCE: No. She didn't, did she? What?

KARIN: I've been two, three times.

MARY: *(Over this)* What bridge?

KARIN: It's just before you get to the house—and it was made of wood—on purpose.

JOYCE: What do you mean?

KARIN: So any automobile crossing it? It would make a lot of noise. Thump-thump-thump... A friend of mine told me this, a guard there had told her—thump thump thump—so all the women who lived there with Eleanor—the ones who made furniture?—would be warned that someone was coming, and so could stop doing whatever they were doing...

(HANNAH *spins the spinner, stopping the conversation. As salad spinner is stopping:)*

HANNAH: *(To KARIN, continuing)* It seemed to be a very different group who go to Val Kill, than to—

JOYCE: I'm sure that's true.

KARIN: You noticed that today?

JOYCE: *(Nods)* Than to Franklin's... We heard one woman tell her woman friend—. *(To HANNAH)* Didn't we?

HANNAH: What are you talking about? Just one more time. Sorry. *(She spins one more time, then as it winds down:)*

JOYCE: This woman was musing that Val Kill might be the only real "monument"?

HANNAH: Oh that. *(She will dry the lettuce with paper towels.)*

GEORGE: *(Looks up from the booklet)* What??

JOYCE: —if that's the word—

MARY: It's not a "monument".

JOYCE: "Official" something—whatever you want to call it, —to a *woman* in all of the United States.

MARY: Betsy Ross?

GEORGE: That's what I was going to say.

MARY: *(Over this)* In Philadelphia, doesn't she have—?

JOYCE: *(Over the end of this)* That's for the flag, Mary. Not for the woman.

KARIN: Maybe it's not true. Still it feels like it's true.

MARY: Some years ago, when we first moved here… Thomas and I went together.

KARIN: To the Roosevelt home?

MARY: *(Nods as)* He asked the guard if he could take his wheelchair up in the little elevator—the one F D R would pull himself up in…

KARIN: Did they let him?

MARY: *(Of course not:)* No…

(HANNAH has gone back to the refrigerator to look for more salad fixings.)

HANNAH: *(To MARY)* Anything you don't want me to use?

(MARY *shakes her head.*)

JOYCE: You going to keep the ramps? Outside? I was surprised the ramps were still up.*(To* "KARIN"*)* George built them.

GEORGE: I'm ready to take them down. I agree, they're in the way…

JOYCE: *(To* KARIN*)* My brother's a carpenter.

KARIN: I know.

(HANNAH *takes a red pepper from the refrigerator.*)

MARY: *(To* HANNAH*)* That's been washed.

HANNAH: Why don't you let George take those ramps away, Mary. He can do it this weekend…

MARY: What if your Mom breaks a leg or something…

JOYCE: She doesn't live here now.

MARY: When she visits… Anyway, there's no rush, is there?

GEORGE: *(Standing up)* Just tell me when…I thought I'd check on Mom. Mary just reminded me that she's still here. I almost forgot.

JOYCE: George, you're just going to wake her up. She'll call us if she needs us… Why cause problems?

(GEORGE *will sit back down.*)

HANNAH: *(As she takes the salad vegetables to the table to cut, to* MARY*)* Those ramps are ugly… Let George get them out of your way. That's not how Thomas would want us to remember him, Mary…

JOYCE: *(To* GEORGE, *to sort of change the subject)* So how's your work going? How's business? I haven't asked.

MARY: *(Happy that the conversation has moved away from her)* He's been working on a big order. A whole dining room set. Table. *(To* HANNAH*)* Sideboard?

HANNAH: Some old tree had fallen on the client's property.

KARIN: What do you mean?

GEORGE: An Ash... A hundred year old ash, at least. Beautiful wood. And so they wanted everything made out of *their* tree. I've been drying all of it. My whole shop is full of ash...

HANNAH: The client told George how much they loved that tree...

JOYCE: *(To* KARIN*)* George makes beautiful furniture.

KARIN: I remember.

MARY: You should peek into his shop sometime.

KARIN: I'd love to.

HANNAH: *(Over this)* He's *already* made some of the furniture...

GEORGE: *(Knows where she is going with this)* I have...

JOYCE: What?

HANNAH: He finally just met the client with the "ash" last week. Until then they'd done everything over the phone. The client closes his house in the winter. But he happens to be up here for something and meets George at his shop. And George has now worked out what he'll charge—

JOYCE: You didn't already have a deal?

GEORGE: I talked to him...

HANNAH: *(Ignoring this)* And right away, the client's "negotiating". The price George has given, you see, is exactly what George wants. No more, no less. He's worked all that out. What he thinks is fair. *(To* GEORGE*)* What you can "live with". What "makes sense". But the client just cuts twenty percent off. Just like that. *(Snaps her finger)* I tell George, but that's what he's *used* to doing. Today everybody *assumes* everybody is negotiating...about every thing. Isn't that true?

JOYCE: I suppose so... Yeh.

KARIN: That's true. Even this job at this school—

GEORGE: I told him I'd take five percent off.

HANNAH: He'd already been working for months; and the guy of course sees this. He's in the shop. So the guy tells George—okay, then if you're not going to "negotiate", then fuck you, truck the wood back to my house. He'll get someone else to make his fucking furniture. *(Then)* George had already begun... He'd dried the wood. Cut the wood. Designed two tables, the desk... He's already built a little coffee table. George had "proudly" showed that to the client when he arrived...

(Then:)

JOYCE: I bet it'll work out. That asshole just enjoys negotiating. He's having fun with you. They just do that instinctively now...

HANNAH: The guy's lawyer has called. "We want the wood."

(They work, then)

JOYCE: Have any of you been up to Hudson recently?

HANNAH: Oh god. What is happening to us? Where do we belong?

KARIN: I haven't been to Hudson.

JOYCE: My boss has a weekend place in Hudson. She is always talking about the parties up there. *(To GEORGE)* When *we* were growing up that place was—*poor.*

HANNAH: No one can live there anymore. No one. *(Another case in point)* Saugerties? Who'd have believed that? George has started calling us—the people who grew up here—he calls us the people of Brigadoon. *(Smiles at* GEORGE*)*

JOYCE: Sounds about right.

HANNAH: You watch the Channel 4 news and weather, and there on the weather map—most nights? *Rhinebeck.* Little bitty Rhinebeck on the New York City news. I guess so the weekenders know what the hell to pack...

MARY: *(Over the end of this)* I'm sure that's why.

KARIN: *(Over this)* I've seen that.

HANNAH: *(To* JOYCE*)* Oh and this you'll enjoy. *(Standing, to* MARY*)* Did I see a cucumber?

MARY: In the back. *(Of the refrigerator)*

GEORGE: *(Same time)* Enjoy what?

HANNAH: *(To* GEORGE*)* Next door. *(Points. She goes to the refrigerator.)*

MARY: That was a long time ago. When I read that, I wasn't that offended —

GEORGE: You didn't grow up here, Mary.

JOYCE: What are you talking about?

*(*HANNAH *will clean the cucumber in the sink; and as they talk, dry it, return the table, peel it, slice it, and add it to the salad:)*

HANNAH: *(To* JOYCE*)* One of the little free papers that are around now—

GEORGE: We had a decent local paper once upon a time.

HANNAH: *(Over this)* They just reprinted last week—I think they found it amusing? An article from back in the '70s; printed excerpts... It had been in *The Times Magazine. (To* MARY*)* You still have your copy?

MARY: If I do—on that pile to recycle. In the dining room.

HANNAH: *(To* JOYCE*)* Your Mom actually remembers the person who wrote it. She lived next door for about a year?

JOYCE: Who?? When?

GEORGE: *(Over this)* You're too young.

HANNAH: She was from Manhattan—and she had rented that house *(To* KARIN*)* that is just next door. Up the hill. She saw herself as some sort of writer— and she wrote about her "year in Rhinebeck". As a transplanted New Yorker? I have to show you... *(Wiping her hands, she goes off to the dining room.)*

GEORGE: I think I sort of remember her.

JOYCE: What did she write?

MARY: *(Over this)* A whole lot of crap.

GEORGE: *(Same time)* Condescending shit. How cute we are. How cute this village is. Its cute people. How— unreal. *(Making his point)* Like Brigadoon... She's from "gritty" "real" Manhattan... And she comes here, and it's quiet, and still, and soooo scary...

JOYCE: Why scary?

KARIN: *(Same time)* Rhinebeck?

GEORGE: It's too clean. Too pretty.

*(*HANNAH *returns with the newspaper:)*

HANNAH: *(Reading)* "...like we're living on the cover of a twenty-five cent Christmas card. The smooth whiteness of it all!" *(To* MARY*)* It was on top.

GEORGE: *(Making a point)* "Whiteness."

KARIN: Was she African American—?

HANNAH: No. *(Obviously)* She was a *New Yorker*...

GEORGE: And then she thinks—Oh she's figured us out... Read that part...

(MARY *covers the ratatouille and goes and stands over them at the table—every now and then she will check on ratatouille.*)

KARIN: *(To* MARY*)* Anything I can—?

(MARY *shakes her head.*)

GEORGE: Read it to Karin.

HANNAH: She doesn't care—

KARIN: I'm interested...I am.

GEORGE: *(Reads over* HANNAH's *shoulder)* Here... "I'll tell you where they are, the blotches and blemishes. They're stashed away in their 'homes.'" Read...

HANNAH: *(Handing him the paper)* Here... You want to read it?

JOYCE: What the hell is she talking about?

GEORGE: She puts "homes" in quotes. I guess they're not *real. (Reads)* "Things are *taken care of* in small towns. Out of the "goodness" of people's hearts—. "Goodness" also in quotes. So that's fake too? Our goodness? *(Continues)* " —moves are made so that little that's ambiguous remains to taunt the intellect... " She's talking about Rhinebeck...

KARIN: Why would they re-publish something from—?

HANNAH: It still strikes a nerve...? Or once again?

GEORGE: *(Reads)* "It's a workingman's town..." Or was.

HANNAH: Still is on most weekdays, at least in the winter...

GEORGE: *(Over this)* "—good, solid, working-class prosperity. Dinner at five, church on Sunday and bed before nine-thirty. At school the kids sing songs from *Mary Poppins* in voices sweet as pipes, and while

discipline's assumed and the walls are graffiti-free,
the children are taught in the old-fashioned way, as
if nothing had happened in the field of education in
the last twenty years. Yet twenty-five percent who
enter Rhinebeck High don't finish. Instead they marry
young..." *(Skips, then)* "In seven months I haven't seen
one cripple, albino, Puerto Rican, nothing to mar the
bland homogeneity of it all. There are no visible poor."
(Closes the newspaper)

HANNAH: Show Karin...

KARIN: Let me see...

(GEORGE hands KARIN the newspaper.)

HANNAH: *(Over this)* Karin, I B M had just closed in
Kingston, in Poughkeepsie. Three huge plants. This
town was dirt poor. And this lady got to live in that big
house on that hill for next to nothing.

MARY: For two hundred a month! She wrote that.

GEORGE: The dripping condescension. Can they even
hear themselves?

HANNAH: Are we just going to bitch in front of Karin?

KARIN: It's fine. Really. Go ahead and bitch... I bitch all
the time.

GEORGE: *(To KARIN, over the end of this)* We work their
land, or mow it; we keep up their properties, we fix
their houses to make life comfortable for them on the
weekends or their summer vacations... We build their
furniture...

*(GEORGE goes to the refrigeator to pour himself another
drink. MARY begins to fill the pasta pot with water from the
sink.)*

JOYCE: An actor friend was telling me—

MARY: *(To JOYCE)* I can't hear. Just a second...

(As the water fills the pot, GEORGE *asks if anyone wants wine. they don't, not yet.)*

(Then, when she can hear:)

MARY: *(To* JOYCE*)* What were you saying?

JOYCE: An actor friend, he was telling me—Karin, I think he might teach at the Atlantic Theater School too—.

HANNAH: *(To* GEORGE*)* Karin teaches there.

JOYCE: *(Over this)* "Henry"…what? What's his last name? I forget.

KARIN: I think I know who you mean. Henry…?

JOYCE: Whatever my good friend's name is, he said—a lot of his friends instead of having the ambition to say, open up a restaurant, with all that overhead, and loans, and banks and stuff. He said, these days, they're going out and getting themselves a food truck. Like that's the height of their ambition now. A food truck.

KARIN: That sort of thing is getting more and more popular.

HANNAH: With kids?

GEORGE: Like peddlers.

KARIN: *(Over this)* No, not just kids.

JOYCE: *(Over the end of this)* Maybe that's what Rhinebeck needs now. Maybe George, you and Hannah should just start up a food truck. Drive it around to the rich people's houses. Ring a bell. Make 'em a nice latte.

GEORGE: We're laughing now…

HANNAH: Who's laughing?

JOYCE: *(Teasing)* I could design you little cute costumes… Both of you.

MARY: *(To* GEORGE*)* We went to an art show at Bard
last fall? Thomas and me… *(To* HANNAH*)* I think
maybe it was one of the last times he went anywhere…

GEORGE: What was the art show?

MARY: Very contemporary. *(To* HANNAH*)* Didn't I tell
you about this?

HANNAH: I don't know.

MARY: Stuff on the floor; videos; things that didn't
make a lot sense… To me. *(Smiles)* We were being
"hip". We're in one room when an elderly African
American man comes in. He's wearing sunglasses, and
he has a white cane.

KARIN: So, blind.

*(*MARY *puts the pasta pot on the stove, and turns on the
burner.)*

MARY: Yeh. And leading him along, guiding him,
I guess, are these two very attractive young white
women, eighteen, nineteen years old. In very short
skirts. It was an odd sight. Thomas right away was
curious. The three went from art piece to art piece;
and the girls would take turns describing to the blind
man what they saw. The colors. Shapes, and so forth.
You couldn't help but hear what they told him; they
spoke in a little louder than normal voice. So everyone
there heard them. *(She goes to the cupboard to get the
box of pasta.)* And you couldn't help but notice that
sometimes, or most of the time, the women would not
really be describing the art piece.

KARIN: What?

MARY: If, say, something were yellow, they'd say it
was red. And they'd also add things that weren't even
there.

GEORGE: *They* were part of the show. They were a piece of art.

MARY: Yes. That's right. George is right. That's just what we realized. Who sees and who doesn't. Who deceives and who is deceived.

Who's dependent on whom for what? Thomas loved it. His favorite thing in the show... *(Explaining why:)* He said whenever he met someone—from Wall Street, with a lot of money—it was always like –

HANNAH: Who would Thomas meet?

MARY: *(Lists)* Board members of theaters—that were doing his plays; or just someone—like George's client. Rich people; really rich people. Up here some days you trip over them. He said it's like talking to someone who speaks a whole other language. But uses the same words...I remember, he said, say one of these people tells you: "the sky is green". But you look at the sky and it's blue. What you see with your own eyes is that it's blue... So you say, "what are you talking about, it's blue." And when you finally get their attention—that's not always so easy he said—it comes out that they've just changed the meaning of "sky". And they think it's their right to do that... See, Thomas said, that's what you're going to be up against...

(Then)

GEORGE: So *they're* the young sexy girls in the mini-skirts, and *we're* the old blind guy being led along, and having everything explained to us...? Sounds about right. I think Thomas got that right... *(Then)* And I can hear him saying that too...

(Then)

HANNAH: Mary told me she didn't want to go to the Roosevelt Museum today, Joyce, because that had been one of Thomas' favorite places.

JOYCE: Uh-huh…

GEORGE: But isn't that why we went? *(To* HANNAH*)* I thought that's why we went. Am I wrong?

HANNAH: *(Continues)* Because… *(To* MARY*)* Okay? You mind? Can I tell them? *(Then)* She's angry at Thomas right now. Right? Really angry. As we were walking back up the hill at the Mills Mansion, back to our cars, Mary told me this. How angry she is at him…

GEORGE: Because he's not here?

HANNAH: I think so.

MARY: It's not rational.

HANNAH: And what is?

JOYCE: I can understand that. I suppose I'm angry at Thomas too.

KARIN: I understand too.

MARY: Left behind… What it feels like. You'd think being a doctor, I'd be a little more rational… *(Then)* Could we talk about something else? I'd really like to talk about something else. And George, I think, I'd like a glass of wine now too.

HANNAH: *(As she looks at her watch)* I'll join Mary. But I want a nice glass, George. A stem glass. A *real* wine glass…

GEORGE: I'm just using—

HANNAH: *(Obviously)* I know what you use…

MARY: Me too. A nice glass.

HANNAH: Mary too.

MARY: *(Over this)* I want a damn nice wine glass too.

HANNAH: *(Explaining to* KARIN*)* The good glasses are in the dining room…

GEORGE: Karin? Wine?

KARIN: No thanks, I'm driving. And I'm sure the last thing you need is to have to put me up for the night.

(GEORGE *heads off into the dining room.*)

MARY: We have room, (*To* HANNAH) don't we?

HANNAH: There's plenty of room.

(MARY *opens the pasta box:*)

JOYCE: I always make too much pasta…

MARY: My mother taught me how to measure. She had a trick. And it works.

JOYCE: What trick?

HANNAH: We'll need a salad dressing, Mary… (*She heads to refrigerator for salad dressing fixings.*)

JOYCE: Can't we just have some Paul Newman—?

MARY: Hannah makes a very nice salad dressing. (*Answering* JOYCE) My mother had this trick. Say pasta for two people… You imagine you have your hand (*Demonstrates*) wrapped around a man's erect penis. Like this. And that's how much pasta. For two. How much pasta…

HANNAH: She's showed me this. It works. I do it all the time now.

(GEORGE *returns with the fancy glasses.*)

GEORGE: Do what all the time?

MARY: (*Ignoring him*) So if it's five or six—then you do it three times.

JOYCE: (*Interested*) Your mother told you that?

HANNAH: It works.

GEORGE: What?

HANNAH: Nothing, George.

(GEORGE *will pour and hand out the wine as:*)

MARY: *(More to the story)* Once I was measuring it out just as my mother'd taught me, you know —. And she was there in the kitchen—and she looks over my shoulder and says—very disparagingly, I thought: "Who have *you* been going out with?"

(The women laugh.)

GEORGE: I don't understand.

JOYCE: Mothers...

GEORGE: What???

HANNAH: Girl talk, George. Never mind.

(Lights fade)

6.
By Bread Alone

(The same, a short time later)

(As HANNAH *prepares her salad dressing; the middle of conversation:)*

GEORGE: We went with Mom to Bread Alone this week...

MARY: *(To* HANNAH*)* Oh, you told me this.

GEORGE: And Peter... *(To* HANNAH*)* what's-his-name?? He's there. Come on, what's his name? You went to school with him. *(To* JOYCE*)* So did you.

JOYCE: Peter—??

KARIN: What's Bread Alone?

JOYCE: *(Over the end this)* A little coffee shop on East Market...

HANNAH: *(To* JOYCE*)* It hasn't changed yet.

GEORGE: He paints houses now. What's-his-name? Why the fuck can't I remember names anymore?

Anyway, he starts telling us—anyone who's in earshot—his "history of our time". That's what he calls it.

JOYCE: What does that mean?

(MARY *is smiling.*)

HANNAH: *(Agreeing with* MARY*)* It is funny....

GEORGE: Everything, he says, every *thing* can be traced back to just—one act.

MARY: *(To* KARIN*)* Anyone talking in any kind of non-whisper and everyone hears it in Bread Alone.

JOYCE: What act?

HANNAH: *(Over this)* That's why everyone goes there, Karin. You really have to watch what you say there.

JOYCE: What act?

MARY: *(Over this)* Especially in the front. The tables are close together in the front. *(To* HANNAH*)* Were you in the front?

HANNAH: We were in the front.

GEORGE: *(Continues over some of this)* Peter what's-his-name is telling everyone how so much of what we now are, what we have now become, and what's now happening to us—can be traced back to one act, during one pizza night, in a small kitchen area, right next to the Oval Office.

JOYCE: *(Getting it, to* KARIN*)* Bill and Monica. We know this. Why do we want to hear this? *(To* MARY*)* You need any help, Mary?

HANNAH: It's funny, Joyce.

GEORGE: We're all listening now. All of recent American "history", he says, is traceable—

JOYCE: Are we still "fascinated" by this??

GEORGE: *(Over this)* —to that one act of—and he lowered his voice so it's even deeper—one act of "fellatio".

JOYCE: And Mom is there with you? Jesus.

GEORGE: Peter what's-his-name says it like it's a musical note: "Fellatio".

HANNAH: George...

GEORGE: "Let us now see just what directly resulted from that late night of pizza, and—and so forth, so many many years ago."

HANNAH: Peter what's-his-name starts listing every terrible thing from the past twenty years.

GEORGE: He lets the "fellatio" settle, and then begins the list: Impeachment. No argument there. *(Next:)* Ending that law that kept the banks from becoming casinos... What was that called?

HANNAH: *(Over the end of this)* Glass something.

JOYCE: Steagall.

OTHERS: Glass Steagall.

(OTHERS: *"We remembered that. We can still remember things!" "If we work together."*)

KARIN: *(Over this)* What does that have to do with—

HANNAH: That's what we all ask.

GEORGE: *(Over this)* He explains, Bill and Hillary, were so worried about going broke—personally—after all, didn't she say "they were dead broke", that's what they thought the Republicans were really after.

JOYCE: And they were. They were. Of course they were.

GEORGE: *(Over this)* To completely bankrupt them. So that's why, according to Peter, Bill felt he sure as hell was going to need some rich friends—so he turns to

Wall Street. And at almost the very last second of his very last days in office, with a stroke of his pen—

HANNAH: *(Explaining)* The banks can become casinos. *(To* JOYCE*)* It's one explanation.

GEORGE: *(The list:)* Next: That really rich guy. Mark...?

HANNAH: Rich.

GEORGE: "Rich." Now I should have remembered that. Mark Rich. Bill helps out this billionaire friend—

KARIN: Didn't Hillary know his wife?

GEORGE: *(Over this)* So maybe later, if Bill needed help... Next: *(Continues list)* Gore lost. When Gore should have won easily. And look what we got. Iraq. *(Continues the list)* The great recession—or as Peter calls it, "the casino goes bust", directly related, we know now, Peter says—to those very same changes Bill made for his new Wall Street buddies. So Peter what's-his-name begins to add it all up: the loss of something like hundreds of thousands of lives; three or four trillion dollars of treasure; millions of homes underwater; foreclosures; bankruptcies, so forth and so on, —all directly traced back to one night of pizza and—and you know what...

JOYCE: Did Mom even understand what he was trying to say?

HANNAH: You mean does she know what the word "fellatio" means?

JOYCE: I guess that's what I'm asking.

HANNAH: I don't know.

JOYCE: Never mind, I don't want to know.

GEORGE: Mom just kept eating her salad, Joyce. I don't know if she understood or not. But Mrs Howard—my fifth grade teacher. She must be ninety now. She was a mean teacher. At least to me. She was there too. *(Incredulous, to* JOYCE*)* She's still alive.

HANNAH: *(To* MARY*)* I forgot to tell you this.

GEORGE: Anyway, once Peter has finished... "that one night of pizza and—fellatio..." For like a minute, Bread Alone is completely silent. You just hear someone behind the counter, grinding coffee. And then, that's when, Mrs Howard takes a sip of her tea, wipes her lips, and says out loud, to the whole silent room: *(In her voice)* "Well, I just hope those two got some pleasure out of it."

(Laughter)

MARY: *(Laughing)* That's not really funny. Mrs Howard is... She's not well, George.

GEORGE: I know. I know.

JOYCE: I didn't know. *(To* HANNAH*)* Mrs Howard knew what it meant.

(As she gets up to put the pasta in and as she shows the women how she has measured out the pasta:)

MARY: Karin, Peter what's-his-name puts his own hand-painted lawn signs all over his front yard about three months before every election. Not for candidates, just for "ideas". He's really pissed off. I suppose it makes him feel better.

JOYCE: It must not have been a weekend at Bread Alone. *(Getting up)* What can I do, Mary?

KARIN: *(To* HANNAH*)* Why? I don't— *(Understand)*

HANNAH: *(Explaining)* We wouldn't talk like that when the weekenders are around, Karin. *(To* JOYCE*)* It was Monday.

(MARY has set the timer.)

MARY: *(To* JOYCE*)* Stir the pasta? *(To the others)* Thomas said to me once—I just remembered this. I keep remembering things...

JOYCE: You said.

HANNAH: *(Over this)* What did Thomas say?

MARY: Thomas told me that years ago, that before the Civil War, slaves were known to do "shows", sort of "plays", behind their cabins. Just for the other slaves. Making "fun" of the masters... Made them feel not alone, he said... Made them feel better...I just thought of that. This *(Us)* —reminded me of that.

(Then)

KARIN: Yesterday, I was talking to a sweet young math teacher. Twenty-three, twenty-four. She's new too. This semester. No one talks to her either. She said she goes home each night and watches both M S N B C and Fox News. Just switches back and forth.

GEORGE: Oh god don't do that. Tell her not to do that.

KARIN: We're asking each other: who is supporting him? Who are they? Does any of this make sense?

JOYCE: What are you—?

HANNAH: The election.

KARIN: We're just sitting in the teacher's lounge. And we both find ourselves saying the same thing—we are so damn confused right now. *(Referring to* MARY*)* I want to feel better.

HANNAH: Our son keeps saying, "feel the Bern, Mom".

GEORGE: I want to be young again...

HANNAH: Paulie says he can still win.

JOYCE: He won Colorado.

GEORGE: *(Repeats)* I want to be young again...

KARIN: This other teacher was saying—what if our side were to fall apart for some reason. Think about that. It's possible. Maybe very possible. Think what we would be left with. It's hard to fathom.

JOYCE: I can't go there. I'm not going there. *(To* HANNAH*)* I just realized what you're saying—Paulie can now vote! My god, I am so fucking old.

KARIN: If our side—falls apart. It could. She could.

JOYCE: No. No.

HANNAH: I know women... Women of a certain age... They really dislike Hillary. I have at least two friends who say they'd never ever vote for her.

MARY: I want to vote for Larry David.

(Laughter and "me too", "I would too")

JOYCE: Why didn't Warren run?

KARIN: Last week I went on a date to this art show. *(To* HANNAH*)* This relates to...

HANNAH: Hillary?

KARIN: *(Over this)* I thought it was a date. Then it wasn't a "date". I'm always making that mistake... It can be so god damn confusing...

HANNAH: *(To* JOYCE*)* Is it for you too?

JOYCE: Can be. Sometimes.

KARIN: We went to a folk art show in some little gallery. He knew the owner. Oh. And this isn't what I was going to tell you. I just remembered: there was a big wooden carved sign, from I think the early 1800s, hanging from the ceiling, a sign for some old inn; of— the Angel *Gabriel.*

JOYCE: That's neat.

KARIN: With his horn. We're all Gabriels. I kept the name, it certainly is a better stage name than "Smith".

(Smiles)

JOYCE: Is that why you kept it?

KARIN: Sort of. What I wanted to say was—a
needlepoint caught my eye—of a "Lady Liberty".
Over two hundred years old. Made just after the
Revolution. And what was so surprising is that in this
needlepoint, Lady Liberty wasn't pictured as some
"ideal woman"—you know, on a cloud, holding a flag,
with young and firm pointy breasts.

JOYCE: Right.

KARIN:—shapely legs. As she usually is.

JOYCE: As *men* paint her, George

GEORGE: I'm not a Neanderthal.

KARIN: *(Over this)* As some "idealized Goddess". No,
this Lady Liberty, she was—kind of normal.

JOYCE: What do you mean?

KARIN: Real. Looked sort of like us. Even had a little
weight on her.

JOYCE: Really…

KARIN: Her dress wasn't "sexy". Just practical. And she
even—get this—was of a certain age…

HANNAH: *(Fact, to* JOYCE*)* A woman made that Lady
Liberty.

JOYCE: Obviously.

KARIN: I thought how interesting. Just after the
Revolution, all that had just happened, and *liberty*,
for this artist—was what? Not some abstract ideal.
Instead, perhaps just a self-portrait. Or maybe a sister
or friend modeled for it. *(Then)* I really would like to
see a woman president in my lifetime. And see what
that feels like. See if it would make any difference
whatsoever. Someone who looked like us.

(Then)

JOYCE: But is *she* that woman?

KARIN: I understand... Fair question.

JOYCE: Maybe it's no longer right to ask that. Maybe we have to stop asking that.

HANNAH: Sometimes I look at Hillary and I see just—a fraud.

KARIN: I know. I know.

JOYCE: Me too.

HANNAH: When I'm catering: I hear some of the people, the "guests" "talk". About doing good things, their causes. And I think they really mean it. They want to do good. And—then you hear them talk about, well...

JOYCE: What?

HANNAH: You just get the feeling, listening to them talk to each other, that they really believe they deserve all they've got. Somehow *earned* it. So they want to do good, *and* they deserve to be rich. Is she like them?

JOYCE: Chelsea's in a ten million dollar apartment.

KARIN: I think it's a house. *(Shrugs)* Why does she laugh so much?

JOYCE: Hillary?

KARIN: *(Over this)* It doesn't sound real, when she laughs.

MARY: Maybe *that* isn't put on. Maybe that's her. *We* laugh...

JOYCE: I know someone with a laugh like that. It can be real.

HANNAH: *(To GEORGE)* And there's Fucking Zephyr Teachout.

KARIN: What—??

GEORGE: *(To* KARIN*)* She's running here for Congress.

KARIN: I didn't know that.

HANNAH: *(Over this)* I voted for "Zephyr Teachout"— against Cuomo. I really liked her. She seemed—real. *(To* KARIN*)* Now, Karin, she's "rented" a house in our district and running to be our congresswoman. She's "lived" here for like six months. On weekends. I thought she was a good woman.

GEORGE: She still could be.

HANNAH: One more weekender, Joyce. They not only want our land, and get us working for them, but now they think we should make them our voice. Can't we speak for ourselves anymore? Aren't we allowed even that anymore?

KARIN: Still, Hillary is a woman.

JOYCE: Is that enough? To be a symbol?

KARIN: Obama?

GEORGE: He's been more than a symbol. Hasn't he?

MARY: After last night, I'd vote for Megyn Kelly.

HANNAH: If she wasn't a Republican.

MARY: *(Over the end of this)* If she wasn't a Republican....

JOYCE: You watched that? How could you watch that?

MARY: *(Over the end of this)* It was Hannah's fault.

GEORGE: *(Over the end of this)* I went to bed.

JOYCE: It sort of feels to me like we're all about to jump off some crazy high cliff. Doesn't it?

KARIN: Yeh. It does.

HANNAH: Jump or be pushed, Joyce?

GEORGE: Shouting: "What about us?" "What about us?"

JOYCE: It feels like a movie. We're just all watching this movie.

GEORGE: Are we in it?

JOYCE: Do you want to be?

HANNAH: A dream.

JOYCE: Nightmare.

HANNAH: *(Over this)* Where there are recognizable "pieces" of things; but put together in ways so they seem—very strange. Don't you feel something really bad is going to happen?

JOYCE: To us?

(Then)

HANNAH: God, it's going to be a very long eight months.

MARY: *(Smiling)* "Oh, but don't give up!"

JOYCE: What?

HANNAH: *(Same time)* Why are you smiling?

MARY: *(Smiles)* "Please, don't give up." That's what Thomas would say to me. I remember after one especially bad day, when I felt hopeless... By now he was pretty hard to understand, but this time, this day, he speaks really clearly. He sits right here. In his chair.

GEORGE: *(In the chair, to KARIN)* This was Thomas' chair.

MARY: He says to me, "Don't give up. Don't give up. Things do happen. They do, Mary." *(Then)* So do we believe him or not?

(Lights fade.)

7.
Wildewoman

(The same; a short time later. Lucius' Wildewoman plays softly on the I-pod dock.)

(MARY in the middle of a story:)

MARY: It was hard to watch. And of course frustrating. Sometimes—and I do mostly think of myself as a pretty good person—but believe me sometimes I had thoughts. Not pretty thoughts. Maybe I even said things to Thomas out of my frustration. I won't tell you what they were. But I'm sorry that I did. Then one day, he's making his way from his chair to the desk. From here to there. When Thomas has gone about two feet, in like five minutes, I just can't watch anymore. So I put on some music. Something my daughter had sent me.

JOYCE: *(To GEORGE and HANNAH)* You know about this?

(They do.)

MARY: I'd had music on before but nothing had ever "happened". *(Smiles)* No "miracle". But this time—Thomas all of a sudden begins to walk across the kitchen—like normal. In normal time. He picks up something on the desk and begins to walk back. I stop the music. And... *(She demonstrates: he moved very slowly.)* I then put on another C D, and another and another. Some work and some don't. We have no idea why. No one knows why. I don't know why. There are these theories about Parkinson's... Anyway I kept adding to the list of *"Thomas' music"*.

(Timer goes off.)

MARY: And so that's all what's on that I-pod now—just the music we found that Thomas somehow for some reason—could walk to... Why?

(No one knows what to say. MARY *goes to pick up the pasta pot.)*

HANNAH: *(To* MARY*)* Bowls or plates, Mary? *(To* GEORGE*)* George...

*(*GEORGE *will help* MARY *with the pasta pot and take it to the sink.)*

MARY: Plates...

HANNAH: Karin, you want to help me?

(The song finishes...)

KARIN: *(To* HANNAH*)* Where...?

HANNAH: *(To* KARIN*)* I'll show you. The cabinet, next to the high boy in the dining room. *(Calls back)* The white set, right? *(To* KARIN*)* That's what they've been using...

*(*HANNAH *and* KARIN *head to the dining room.* JOYCE *opens the drawer in the table to take out silverware.)*

MARY: There are some lovely napkins... We haven't used them for a while. Not since your mother moved... I was thinking we'd use them tonight. It is a special night... They're in the cabinet out here. I happened to see them. *(Goes to the mudroom)*

JOYCE: *(To* GEORGE*)* You think Mom is going to eat with us? How many are we going to be?

*(*GEORGE *oils the pasta at the sink.)*

GEORGE: We'd better wake her up. She'd be really upset, if we didn't try and wake her up... When does she get to see you?

JOYCE: *(Taking out the silverware)* So we'll be six, you think? Do we still have that much silverware that matches?

GEORGE: Does it matter?

JOYCE: We used to... *(She counts the silverware.)*

MARY: *(Returning with the napkins)* These are nice.
They're old. Your mother found them in the basement;
when we were packing her things...

JOYCE: I don't even remember those.

MARY: She thinks they're from Austria. From relatives.

*(GEORGE, cleaning up, has picked up a couple of Thomas'
old cookbooks from the table:)*

GEORGE: Look, he used postcards for bookmarks.

MARY: What's that one of?

GEORGE: *(Shows)* A woman hanging laundry...

JOYCE: Let me see.

(GEORGE shows JOYCE.)

MARY: Thomas liked pictures of people doing very
simple things. I remember: a woman with a broom.
Another: someone writing a letter. Hammershoi. You
know him? Women with their backs to us. Chardin?
Those two were his favorites. Why?

HANNAH: *(Returning with KARIN)* Mary, the blue table
cloth? That's special, isn't it?...

MARY: That's good.

HANNAH: I took it out.

JOYCE: Mary was just saying today is special...

KARIN: Then we'll put the blue one on? Want me to
do that? I can do that... *(She starts to go:)* What can I
take—?

HANNAH: The salad dressing...

KARIN: Mary, I was looking out the dining room
window at your back yard, just now.

MARY: In the dark?

KARIN: You can't see much now, you're right. But I remember coming up and visiting here. So many years ago. And seeing that stream...

HANNAH: Landsman Kill.

KARIN: And Crystal Lake. Thomas always used to say to me after one of our visits back here—how lucky he was to grow up in Rhinebeck. *(She heads off with the salad dressing.)*

MARY: She's been fine. Hasn't she? No problem at all, Hannah. She seems a little lonely.

HANNAH: She's thinking of staying the night...

JOYCE: I don't think so. No.

MARY: She's got to get back she said.

HANNAH: She just told me she's thinking about it. She's very "tempted" she said... *(To MARY)* She thinks you invited her.

MARY: Did I do that? Did I?

GEORGE: I will go and wake up Mom... Unless, Joyce, you'd rather... *(He smiles and heads off.)*

JOYCE: Fuck you.

GEORGE: Maybe she's not even hungry... *(He is gone.)*

MARY: By the way, Hannah, I know that you, or maybe George, got my daughter to call me today. "Reminded" her to call me. What did you do, phone her, text her? Thank you. I appreciate that... Don't tell George I know. *(To herself)* I'll put the apple crisp in while we eat. *(She will set the oven, and begin the final preparations of the apple crisp.)*

(As HANNAH and JOYCE collect things to take to the dining room:)

JOYCE: I would really like to sit down with Mom sometime and ask her things.

HANNAH: What things?

JOYCE: When I get back. Maybe when I'm back from London, I'll spend more time up here with Mom.

HANNAH: I think she'd like that. Don't you, Mary?

MARY: I know she would...

JOYCE: Today, at the museum... And please don't hate me for saying this... Don't tell George this either. She kept touching me. I know she so wanted me to touch her back. But I found that really hard to do. I don't like touching her. I know that's awful.

(Then)

HANNAH: *(To* JOYCE*)* What would you want to ask her?

JOYCE: *(Shrugs)* So many things. Some of them are just stupid. Once Mom lost her wedding ring? She found it, because she told us she'd dreamed of seeing it by the side of our stream. Next to the weeping willow. And so in the morning, still in her nightgown, she put on boots and went out into the rain, and there it was—just as she had dreamed it. Did she make that up? *(Another one)* She always knows moments before any of us calls, who is calling.

HANNAH: That's what she says...

JOYCE: I feel like I'm fourteen years old when I'm in this house... *(Sees* GEORGE *and* PATRICIA *arriving)* You're awake. She's awake...

*(*GEORGE *appears with his mother,* PATRICIA, *81 years old. She has just been woken up, and so a little confused. everyone speaks louder when they talk to* PATRICIA.*)*

GEORGE: *(Helping her in)* Mom was just telling me a story about Thomas as a little kid. I'd never heard this, Mom.

PATRICIA: I just remembered it. I don't know why...?

JOYCE: Because of today, Mom. What we did this morning. Thomas' ashes…

PATRICIA: Maybe.

HANNAH: What story, Patricia?

PATRICIA: You're cooking? You should have let me help.

HANNAH: It's all ready, Patricia.

PATRICIA: What plates are you using—?

HANNAH: *(Over the end of this, of course:)* The *white* ones.

JOYCE: What story, Mom?

GEORGE: *(To* PATRICIA*)* You want to sit down? She just woke up.

PATRICIA: I thought we were eating dinner?

JOYCE: We are, Mom.

PATRICIA: *(Insisting)* In the dining room.

JOYCE: Yes… Where else?

*(*KARIN *has just returned,* PATRICIA *is looking at her.)*

HANNAH: It's Karin. Thomas' first wife. She came for today. We invited her. Our guest.

GEORGE: She's been here all day.

HANNAH: *(To* GEORGE*)* And she might stay the night…

KARIN: You told me about voting for Roosevelt, Patricia.

PATRICIA: *(Defending herself)* I just woke up. *(To* MARY*)* What can I do?

MARY: I think everything's under control. I think dinner is ready.

PATRICIA: *(Back to* KARIN*, to* MARY*)* And you two get along?

MARY: I was the third wife, Patricia. There was one in between us. We both hate her…

PATRICIA: What can I take in?

JOYCE: What story, Mom? *(To* GEORGE*)* What story?

PATRICIA: *(Ignoring* JOYCE*)* Give me something.

HANNAH: What can she take?

JOYCE: *(Over this)* I think we're fine, Mom.

GEORGE: *(Answering* JOYCE's *question)* Thomas is about two years old and in diapers. And Mom is by herself for some reason—and taking him on an airplane somewhere. You don't remember where, right? This was in the fifties—so a propeller plane.

(Seeing the silverware in JOYCE's *hands:)*

PATRICIA: Where's the good silverware?

JOYCE: What's the good silverware, Mom? This is the only silverware I remember ever using.

MARY: Patricia, that is our good silverware.

PATRICIA: Is it?

GEORGE: *(Continues)* And they're in the air, and Mom smells that Thomas has pooped in his diaper. So she starts to pick him up off his seat, to walk him to the bathroom, to change him, but he pulls his hand away, gets into the aisle, and somehow rips off his shit-filled diaper and starts running down the aisle swinging it.

KARIN: *(Laughing)* Oh my god…!

GEORGE: Thomas' shit flying everywhere!

(They laugh.)

PATRICIA: I wanted to kill him. And for one moment, I opened up my magazine and pretended he wasn't mine.

(She and they laugh.)

PATRICIA: But that didn't last long. You soon realize you don't have a choice. We don't have another set of silverware?

GEORGE: I think we got rid of that years ago, Mom.

PATRICIA: I thought because of today...

GEORGE: I know. But it's gone. It's gone.

MARY: Everyone—take something. I'm just finishing up Thomas' apple crisp.

PATRICIA: What can I do? I want to do something...

KARIN: *(To anyone)* Maybe I *could* stay the night. Let me think...

HANNAH: Here, Patricia, you can carry in the salad. Let me just clean this off...

(As they pick up things, pitcher of water, the salad dressing, etc:)

GEORGE: *(To* JOYCE*)* What time's your train tomorrow?

JOYCE: Early.

KARIN: I've got the wine and the water pitcher... *(She heads off.)* I don't think I had any lunch. I forgot to have lunch.

GEORGE: And I haven't even asked—what's the show you're designing in London?

JOYCE: I'm not the designer, I'm the associate... My boss is "busy". *Die Fledermaus.*

PATRICIA: She's just the assistant, George.

JOYCE: Thanks, Mom.

*(*GEORGE *has the large frying pan of ratatouille:)*

GEORGE: *(To* JOYCE*)* Costumes for that should be fun. You'll have fun. London's always fun, right? *(He heads off.)*

HANNAH: *(Handing her the salad bowl)* Here, Patricia.
You can take this in. I have your arm, Patricia.

PATRICIA: I don't need help. I don't need you to hold
my arm.

HANNAH: Mary, the salt and pepper.

PATRICIA: I'll get it.

HANNAH: Patricia...

(PATRICIA goes back to the table for the salt and pepper.)

PATRICIA: You know what I like to do when I travel?

HANNAH: You want help? That's a lot to carry.

JOYCE: When do you travel now, Mom?

PATRICIA: *(Ignoring her)* To foreign countries. I like to
visit their grocery stores. I find that so interesting. You
should do that. *(Explaining)* What do they have that we
don't. What's the same...

JOYCE: I'm not sure, Mom, I will have time for grocery
stores.

HANNAH: *(To PATRICIA)* Let me help you...

PATRICIA: Joyce can help me. Joyce, hold onto my
arm...

HANNAH: Mary, I've got the pasta...

(JOYCE first goes to wash her hands in the sink:)

PATRICIA: *(To JOYCE)* How long will you be gone?

JOYCE: Not that long, Mom... George and Hannah are
here. And Mary...

(HANNAH heads off.)

PATRICIA: Mary's going to move to Pittsburgh... Her
daughter is there.

JOYCE: I know.

PATRICIA: She's got no one left to take care of here.

JOYCE: I know. *(Holding her as they go)* I'll bet you'll hardly know that I was even gone.

PATRICIA: I doubt that...

JOYCE: *(Heading off)* I got you, Mom. I got you... Hold on to me... I'll be back. I am coming back. Are you hungry, Mom?

(They are gone.)

(MARY is alone.)

MARY: *(To "Thomas")* Your apple crisp...

(Music: Lucius' Wildewoman from the theater speakers.)

(MARY puts the apple crips in the oven. Looks over the kitchen: at Thomas's chair, at the journey he made from chair to desk.)

(Then she picks up the bread, and goes to join the others in the diningroom.)

END OF PLAY

NOTE

I consulted and read numerous books while
writing **Hungry**; the most useful are the following:
Jean Anthelme Brillat-Savarin's extraordinary
**The Physiology of Taste Or Meditations on
Transcendental Gastronomy**; M F K Fisher's **The Art
of Eating**; Priscilla Parkhurst Ferguson's **Accounting
for Taste**; Mrs. Child's **The American Frugal
Housewife** (1833); Laurie Colwin's **Home Cooking**
and **More Home Cooking**; Luke Barr's **Provence, 1970**;
Anne Hollander's **Feeding the Eye**; Matt Taibbi's **The
Divide**; Laurence Tribe and Joshua Matz's **Uncertain
Justice**; Michael Lewis' **Flashboys** (which both Hannah
and Thomas/Mary must have been reading; the former
tries to quote from when he talks about the vultures on
the savannah, and the latter when a blue sky is called
green); Stacy C. Hollander and Valerie Rousseau's
**Self-Taught Genius: Treasures from the American
Folk Art Museum**; Elizabeth Warren's **A Fighting
Chance**; Rand Paul's **Government Bullies**; Mark
Leibovich's **This Town**; Edward M. Smith's **History
of Rhinebeck**. Among the articles I consulted was
Jeff Gordinier's "A Confidante in the Kitchen: Laurie
Colwin used simple…", *The New York Times*, April 2,
2104.

The piece from *The New York Times Magazine* which
is quoted from in Scene 6 is "Getting Out" by Colette
Dowling (March 28, 1976.)

The gift Joyce has bought Mary at Val Kill is **Cookies for Eleanor** by Chandler Roosevelt Lindsey.

In Scene 3, my characters read extensively from Marion Harland's nineteenth century **Common Sense in the Household: A Manual for Practical Housewifery.**

I also found the following interview very helpful: Priscilla Parkhurst Ferguson on the Criterion D V D of the film **Babette's Feast.**

Hungry is a play and a work of fiction, and is not based upon any living person or persons.

R N / Rhinebeck